CLASSICS IN EDUCATION
Lawrence A. Cremin, General Editor

☆ ☆ ☆

Number 1
THE REPUBLIC AND THE SCHOOL
Horace Mann on the Education of Free Men
Edited by Lawrence A. Cremin

Number 2
AMERICAN IDEAS ABOUT ADULT EDUCATION
1710–1951
Edited by C. Hartley Grattan

Number 3
DEWEY ON EDUCATION
Selections with an Introduction and Notes
by Martin S. Dworkin

Number 4
THE SUPREME COURT AND EDUCATION
Edited by David Fellman

Number 5
INTERNATIONAL EDUCATION
A Documentary History
Edited by David G. Scanlon

Number 6
CRUSADE AGAINST IGNORANCE
Thomas Jefferson on Education
Edited by Gordon C. Lee

Number 7
CHINESE EDUCATION UNDER COMMUNISM
Edited by Chang-Tu Hu

Number 8
CHARLES W. ELIOT AND POPULAR EDUCATION
Edited by Edward A. Krug

Number 9

WILLIAM T. HARRIS ON
EDUCATION
(in preparation)
Edited by Martin S. Dworkin

Number 10

THE *EMILE* OF JEAN JACQUES
ROUSSEAU
Selections
Translated and Edited by William Boyd

Number 11

THE MINOR EDUCATIONAL
WRITINGS OF JEAN JACQUES
ROUSSEAU
Selections
Translated by William Boyd

Number 12

PSYCHOLOGY AND THE SCIENCE OF
EDUCATION
Selected Writings of Edward L. Thorndike
Edited by Geraldine M. Joncich

Number 13

THE NEW–ENGLAND PRIMER
Edited by Paul Leicester Ford

Number 14

BENJAMIN FRANKLIN ON
EDUCATION
Edited by John Hardin Best

Number 15

THE COLLEGES AND THE PUBLIC
1787–1862
Edited by Theodore Rawson Crane

Number 17

NOAH WEBSTER'S
AMERICAN SPELLING BOOK
With an Introductory Essay
by Henry Steele Commager

The Colleges
and
The Public, 1787–1862

Edited, with an Introduction and Notes, by

THEODORE RAWSON CRANE

CLASSICS IN

No. 15

EDUCATION

BUREAU OF PUBLICATIONS
TEACHERS COLLEGE, COLUMBIA UNIVERSITY
NEW YORK

© 1963 by Theodore Rawson Crane

Library of Congress Catalog Card
Number 63-9583

The illustration which appears on the cover
of the paperbound edition and on the jacket of
the clothbound edition is a portion of the
frontispiece from *History of Brown University,
with Illustrative Documents* by Reuben Ald-
ridge Guild (1867).

Printed in the United States of America
by the William Byrd Press, Inc.
Richmond, Virginia

Preface

That the period between the Revolution and the Civil War witnessed a marked change in the character of American higher education is now something of a commonplace among historians. Donald G. Tewksbury, in his classic study of *The Founding of American Colleges and Universities Before the Civil War* (1932), located as many as 172 permanent institutions established between 1780 and 1861, and there were hundreds of others that flourished for a time and then died. Moreover, the multiplication of institutions was merely one facet of a larger change that was both more subtle and more pervasive. In the first place, the very participation of greater numbers of students in the collegiate experience was bound to work a transforming influence on that experience, as inevitably the colleges changed to suit their clientele. Then, too, the same currents in American life that had brought the colleges into being—notably, evangelical Protestantism and popular democracy—continued to influence the colleges once they were under way. In responding to such influence, American higher education underwent a radical readjustment.

The nature of this readjustment and its significance for American life at large have been interpreted quite differently in the standard literature on the subject. R. Freeman Butts, for example, whose work *The College Charts Its Course* (1939) dominated the outlook of the 1940's, tended to view the pre-Civil War period largely as an age of reform in higher education. Writing with the optimism so characteristic of educational thought in the thirties, Professor Butts emphasized the number of institutions that engaged in bold and imaginative experiment. Starting with the work of Thomas Jefferson at the University of Virginia and George Ticknor at Harvard, he catalogued a host of proposals reflecting a growing dissatisfaction with the narrowness and provincialism of the traditional classical curriculum. And in such characteristic innovations as the "parallel course" and the independent scientific or technical school, he

v

saw a praiseworthy response to the demands of the utilitarian, democratic society that was coming into being.

More recent historiography, exemplified best in the work of Richard Hofstadter, has tended to take a more pessimistic view of the pre-Civil War colleges. Critical of the effort to popularize higher education in a frontier society, Professor Hofstadter contends in *The Development of Academic Freedom in the United States* (1955) that the early nineteenth century witnessed a vast deterioration in quality, occasioned principally by the crippling forces of denominationalism and equalitarianism. The "great retrogression," as he calls it, affected every aspect of collegiate life: academic standards were low; teaching was atrocious; libraries were inadequate; student discipline was stern; and worst of all, severe strictures on the freedom of scholars prevented the development of advanced university studies. Here was the price paid for the early popularization of higher education; and it is Professor Hofstadter's view that the cost was much too high, that the consequences of nineteenth-century democracy for higher education were, on the whole, deleterious.

Professor Crane's effort in the present volume is somehow to reconcile these two divergent views. Granting the serious limitations of American higher education in the ante-bellum period, he nevertheless points out that the old-time college provided certain educational advantages that the great universities of the twentieth century have yet to duplicate. Moreover, he suggests that many features of the modern university have their source in the educational debates of the mid-nineteenth century, and that some of the collegiate reforms of the past seventy-five years were well under way before the Civil War. Finally, he reminds us that, like it or not, we remain the heirs of many a conflict that was never fully resolved in the ante-bellum discussions; hence, the continuing relevance of the pre-Civil War literature. As Santayana once counseled, those who ignore history are condemned to repeat it.

LAWRENCE A. CREMIN

Contents

TO BUILD AN AMERICAN UNIVERSITY
by Theodore Rawson Crane   1

1. GEORGE WASHINGTON ON A NATIONAL UNIVERSITY (1795)   34

2. THOMAS JEFFERSON ON HIGHER EDUCATION IN VIRGINIA (1814)   37

3. WILLIAM B. ROGERS ON THE UNIVERSITY OF VIRGINIA (1845)   45

4. A MASSACHUSETTS FARMER ON LEARNING AND THE PROFESSIONS: WILLIAM MANNING, *The Key of Libberty* (1798)   52

5. THE DARTMOUTH COLLEGE CASE
ISAAC HILL (1815)   61
WILLIAM PLUMER (1816)   64
JOHN MARSHALL (1819)   67

6. GEORGE TICKNOR: *Remarks on Changes Lately Proposed or Adopted, in Harvard University* (1825)   76

7. THE YALE REPORT (1828)   83

8. DENOMINATIONALISM: WILLIAM S. TYLER, *Prayer for Colleges* (1855)   100

9. FRANCIS WAYLAND
Thoughts on the Present Collegiate System (1842)   112
Report to the Corporation of Brown University (1850)   135

10. HENRY PHILIP TAPPAN
INAUGURAL DISCOURSE (1852)   147
WILBUR F. STOREY'S EDITORIAL ASSAULT ON TAPPAN (1853)   168

11. JONATHAN BALDWIN TURNER: *Plan for an Industrial University, for the State of Illinois* (1851)   172

12. THE MORRILL ACT (1862)   190

The Colleges and the Public
1787–1862

It is these arbitrary lords and petty tyrants, who have done that for their states, which United America will not do for herself. And there is scarce a little princedom, in the Germanic body, which has not contributed more to the amount of human knowledge, and the progress of the human mind, than all that vast empire, which God has given us to administer. Or if we will go back yet three or four centuries, to the foundation of the older universities, we trace them to the bounty of bishops, and cardinals, and popes, and catholic priests; who, if they extorted money from the people by practising on their credulity, knew, at least, how to make some applications of it, which might serve as a lesson to our enlightened land. . . . Our mouths are filled with the praises of our own illumination, we call ourselves happy, and we feel ourselves free, but content with a vulgar happiness, and an inglorious freedom, we leave it to despots, to build universities as the toys and playthings of their slaves.

—EDWARD EVERETT (1820)[1]

Colleges rise up like mushrooms in our luxuriant soil. They are duly lauded and puffed for a day; and then they sink to be heard of no more. Do our wise men fancy, that, by the magic of a technical parchment, they can instantly convert a school or academy, with its master and usher, into a college—where the liberal arts and sciences shall be adequately and thoroughly taught? If so, why not transform at once every grammar school in the State into a college; and thus bring the means of a liberal education to the door of every poor man's cottage? Already, Western colleges, thus established, have become the objects of ridicule and contempt in every enlightened corner of the land.   —PHILIP LINDSLEY (1829)[2]

[1] "Review of Proceedings and Report of the Commissioners for the University of Virginia, presented 8th of December 1818," *North American Review*, Vol. X (January 1820), 133.

[2] "Baccalaureate Address, at Cumberland College, 1829," in *Educational Discourses* (Philadelphia: J. B. Lippincott & Co.; Nashville: W. T. Berry & Co., 1859), p. 161.

But we are told that there are too many colleges; and that this result is due to the voluntary system. In a free country, how can this be helped? There are just now too many banks, too many railroads, too many ships, too much iron; but the law of supply and demand is the only possible corrective for the evil. If a college attracts to itself patronage and endowment, it has a right to live; if it does not, it will die. The law of natural selection applies to colleges as well as to the animal and vegetable world. A college that does good work creates its own patronage by its elevating influence over the community around it. Time alone can determine whether a college has a right to live. —MARTIN BREWER ANDERSON (1876)[3]

3 *Voluntaryism in Higher Education: A Paper Read Before the New York Convocation of Teachers in Albany, July 14, 1876* (New York: Sheldon and Company, 1877), pp. 14–15.

To Build an American University

By THEODORE RAWSON CRANE

I

The pre-Civil War period was emphatically the age of the college, as the period since 1865 has been dominated by the large university. It was a time of incredible expansion: Donald Tewksbury has catalogued nearly 160 permanent institutions established between 1799 and 1861; four times that many had been unsuccessfully projected.[1] But it was also an age of declining educational quality. The patriotic inspiration of the Revolutionary era, the reaction of evangelical Protestantism to eighteenth-century rationalism and deism, the westward movement, local pride, sectional rivalry, and a growing concern for individual opportunity—all these operated to multiply the number of colleges rather than to improve educational standards. Because the country was oversupplied with institutions, colleges competed for patronage with an intensity that merited President Anderson's Darwinian analogies, and their rivalries involved important issues, political and social, as well as academic. The outcome of the competition was important, for in this period, as in every other, the influence of American higher education depended upon the prosperity of individual institutions. Indeed, educational historians might profitably analyze more searchingly the factors which affected the growth

[1] Donald G. Tewksbury, *The Founding of American Colleges and Universities Before the Civil War, With Particular Reference to the Religious Influences Bearing on the College Movement* (New York: Bureau of Publications, Teachers College, Columbia University, 1932).

or decline of influential institutions or particular types of colleges, for there are valuable insights to be gained from a close scrutiny of crucial local developments, insights which are often missed in broader surveys of curricular expansion, the rise of the elective system, or the origins of the graduate school.[2]

In the early national period scholarship and liberal education were seldom considered as worth-while goals in themselves, but rather as means to other objectives. This is hardly surprising in a pioneer society; even in the seaboard regions most Americans were concerned primarily with material advancement. Conspicuous devotion to scholarly excellence was largely limited to institutions

---

[2] R. Freeman Butts, in *The College Charts Its Course: Historical Conceptions and Current Proposals* (New York: McGraw-Hill Book Company, 1939), discusses university development largely in terms of the elective system *versus* prescription; Richard J. Storr, in *The Beginnings of Graduate Education in America* (Chicago: University of Chicago Press, 1953), surveys numerous projects for collegiate reform, stressing their contributions to the idea of education beyond the bachelor's degree. Recent works on American higher education of value to the student of institutional development and the social history of education are Richard Hofstadter and C. De Witt Hardy, *The Development and Scope of Higher Education in the United States* (New York: Columbia University Press, 1952); Richard Hofstadter and Walter P. Metzger, *The Development of Academic Freedom in the United States* (New York: Columbia University Press, 1955); George P. Schmidt, *The Liberal Arts College: A Chapter in American Cultural History* (New Brunswick, New Jersey: Rutgers University Press, 1957); John S. Brubacher and Willis Rudy, *Higher Education in Transition: An American History: 1636–1956* (New York: Harper & Brothers, 1958); and Frederick Rudolph, *The American College and University: A History* (New York: Alfred A. Knopf, Inc., 1962); of these the works of Rudolph and Hofstadter and his collaborators are most rewarding. All these studies are largely dependent on secondary works, especially institutional histories, which vary vastly in quality. Two of the most interesting for the social historian are Robert Samuel Fletcher, *A History of Oberlin College from Its Foundation Through the Civil War* (2 vols.; Oberlin, Ohio: Oberlin College, 1943), and Frederick Rudolph, *Mark Hopkins and the Log: Williams College, 1836–1872* (New Haven: Yale University Press, 1956). Richard Hofstadter and Wilson Smith, eds., in *American Higher Education: A Documentary History* (2 vols.; Chicago: University of Chicago Press, 1961), promise to stimulate new interest in the original sources of American collegiate history.

supported by a stable constituency, including local aristocracies willing to subsidize the indispensable elements of a learned institution, e.g., libraries, scientific equipment, and endowed professorships. The "great retrogression" of the early nineteenth century was the product of genuinely popular forces: sectarian zeal, local pride, antimonopoly movements, and a fierce equalitarianism jealous of intellectual distinction.

Yet it would be wrong to disparage this period excessively. There are elements of the old-time college, such as its common curriculum, combining intellectual training with character building, for which the modern university has produced no adequate substitute. Despite the limitations which their social setting imposed on American colleges, a prophetic group of leaders foresaw the emergence of great universities. Some were pragmatists, others idealists; some were scholars and others primarily moralists. Generally, however, they were aware that in order to succeed, American universities would have to serve the needs of a society of free and aspiring citizens.

At least three general sources of instability confronted American colleges before 1860. A world-wide intellectual and technological revolution precipitated by discoveries in the natural sciences threatened to destroy the unity of the traditional college curriculum, which was rooted in the Middle Ages. Rising equalitarianism in American society demanded that colleges serve a wider constituency. Though the colleges were increasingly characterized by their critics as "aristocratic," access to the three learned professions—law, medicine, and the ministry—to which they had traditionally catered was less dependent than previously on formal academic preparation; and the vocationalism that pervades higher education today was slow to win acceptance, for the Jacksonian age distrusted expertise of any sort. Meanwhile, population growth and the westward movement gave rise to an excessive proliferation of institutions, stimulated by the universal American booster spirit and the competition of religious denominations.

To some extent the American college had always been

a frontier institution: colonial Harvard and Dartmouth, for example, were established in newly founded communities. At no period, however, were all institutions located on the outskirts of settlement. More significantly, the American college stood on the frontier between New World promise and Old World achievement, the former expressed in aspirations for material growth and social opportunity, the latter in the form of traditional institutions and inherited cultural values. In this situation Americans were ambivalent. Many condemned Old World traditions, but others turned naturally to European models in creating monuments or symbols of their country's greatness.[3] Most citizens, increasingly confident of the strength of their political system and of the opportunities offered by their mobile society, insisted that their cultural institutions needed no improvement. A minority with leisure for study, reflection, or foreign travel knew better; but when they confronted their countrymen with evidence of national deficiencies, they were compelled to eulogize European achievements. Such appeals had little effect on the average American.

Thus, institutional development proceeded piecemeal and was characterized by many false starts and overambitious proposals during a period when most colleges led a precarious existence. Land, buildings, and minimal endowment were often easier to come by than a sufficient number of pupils. No other feature of the American college system before 1860 contrasts more fundamentally with the present. It was against the background of a chronic shortage of adequately prepared students, willing to invest time and money in academic studies and to sacrifice countless immediate rewards, that projects for educational reform were debated. Institutions could not survive without students; hence, educators were frequently forced to reconsider their objectives. What bargains might be offered to attract pupils? What innovations would fatally compromise the principles for which

3 See Max Lerner, "The Slaying of the European Father," in *America as a Civilization* (New York: Simon and Schuster, 1957), Chapter 1, Section 3.

colleges stood? Sincere and able men differed profoundly on these matters.

In the struggle for survival colleges often modified drastically their expressed objectives and purposes. Both the denominational schools advocated by militant sectarians and the religiously neutral public institutions envisaged by Thomas Jefferson, Philip Lindsley, and Henry Philip Tappan were moderated by necessity. Advocates of church colleges urged their coreligionists to sustain schools where the sons of the faithful could be educated within the fold, while, at the same time, they assured the public that young gentlemen of all Christian persuasions were welcome in an atmosphere free of efforts to proselytize. Meanwhile, most early state universities conformed to religious pressures; generally they differed little in appearance from sectarian colleges, employing clerical presidents and professors, and occasionally distributing faculty chairs among major denominations. The divergent ideals which impelled the multiplication of sectarian institutions on the one hand, and the separation of public and private colleges on the other, were seldom realized in practice.

European universities stood at the summit of an adequate structure of preparatory institutions, but Americans—New Englanders were an exception—preferred to establish infant universities rather than academies or high schools to supply them with qualified matriculants. A college sounded more imposing than a preparatory school, though many so-called colleges were little better than academies. Sensitive to the charge that colleges were "aristocratic," faculties admitted many poorly prepared students. Stated entrance requirements were low, and much of the college course was on a level with the present-day high school program. Nineteenth-century critics familiar with European conditions noted that American institutions, whether they called themselves colleges or universities, were in fact inferior approximations of the German *gymnasium*. The development of true universities would require higher standards and more advanced courses than American colleges could afford.

Most institutions were compelled to follow financial policies which made real quality impossible. After acquiring a site and erecting one or more buildings, usually dormitories, they were forced to charge the lowest possible tuition. As a result, libraries and other educational facilities were woefully inadequate, and faculties were chronically underpaid.[4] "The founding of a college," wrote Francis Wayland in 1842, "consists not so much in providing means for higher education . . . as the collecting of funds for eleemosynary distribution."

The most perceptive critics—such men as Thomas Jefferson, George Ticknor, Francis Wayland, and Henry Philip Tappan—were deeply concerned with these compromises of principle and purpose. Starting with ideals of thorough teaching, scholarly achievement, or institutional greatness, willing or even eager to measure American inadequacies by European achievements, they advocated fundamental changes in the structure and practices of American colleges as steps toward permanent improvement. Significantly, almost every specific reform they proposed met with bitter resistance. The common elements of the collegiate system were everywhere defended as immutable.[5] In vain did Francis Wayland point out that the only universal significance of the bachelor's degree was "a residence of four years, and the payment of the college bills." Sarcastically Henry Philip Tappan observed that "In creating Colleges, we have uniformly begun with two things—the erection of dormitories, and a commencement Exhibition: As if sleeping in cloisters,

4 See Frederick Rudolph, "Who Paid the Bills?" *Harvard Educational Review*, XXXI, Spring 1961, 144–157.

5 The four-year collegiate course was entirely or almost entirely prescribed with heavy emphasis on Latin, Greek, and mathematics, plus rhetoric and declamation, a smattering of descriptive instruction in several natural sciences, and in the senior year a course in moral and intellectual philosophy often taught by the president. Students who pursued this course received the A.B. degree. The A.M. was granted automatically to alumni of good character three years or more after graduation upon application and payment of appropriate fees. American colleges almost universally housed their students in barrack-like dormitories intended as an equivalent for the English residential college.

reciting poems and orations in public, and the conferring of degrees, were essential to the Educational System." To most educators they *were* essential. The majority of officers in pre-Civil War institutions were not interested in copying European universities which they had never seen, for they were too deeply involved in the immediate tasks of instruction and discipline. They were primarily pedagogues and guardians of youth, and only secondarily scholars or patrons of higher learning; and the imperatives of their daily routine shaped their educational philosophy.

Even the critics were preoccupied with the limitations imposed by the collegiate setting. George Ticknor, who hoped to transplant the free electives and high scholarship of European universities to America, began by insisting that student morale must be improved and thorough teaching made a cynosure. Francis Wayland, advocate of free electives and alternative degrees, and critic of the residential college, more than once sacrificed elements of institutional strength to what he conceived to be the requirements of an effective disciplinary system. Routine problems loomed large because colleges were chiefly attended by immature adolescents. Public opinion reacted far more critically to disciplinary crises than to intellectual deficiencies. Faculties and trustees, predominantly drawn from clerical circles, took their moral responsibilities with the utmost seriousness.

Other more distinctively intellectual features of the traditional system were defended with equal zeal, however. Few colleges dared to lengthen the four-year course, buttressed by precedent and common custom. At the University of Virginia, which had abolished traditional degrees, the average length of student residence in 1845 was less than two years, a fact that afforded little encouragement to reformers who hoped to develop universities by adding graduate studies to the required undergraduate course. In other universities, the bachelor's degree was the universal reward for students who persevered through four years of study. Since the Middle Ages it had symbolized an apprenticeship in the liberal arts.

In America it remained largely immune to modification, a badge of equality for the struggling frontier college which aspired to become a western Yale. Few reformers —Thomas Jefferson, Eliphalet Nott, and Francis Wayland were exceptions—dared to alter the definition of the baccalaureate degree, and proposals for an earned master's degree, a step toward graduate education, were premature before 1860. Most colleges were unwilling to do more than provide occasional elective options within the standard undergraduate course, or to advertise that pupils unwilling to pursue the whole program might pursue a "partial" course for which no degree was granted. Such special courses, however, were poorly patronized. Though the number of Americans who sought a college education was discouragingly small, those who did enroll usually desired a recognized degree. Only after the Civil War did "Bachelor of Science" and "Bachelor of Philosophy" degrees win acceptance, and only then was graduate education really feasible. The prevailing conservative attitude toward degrees is significant. The determination with which college officers defended the traditional baccalaureate was the educational equivalent of the national fetish for legal and constitutional restraints on the restless energies of a pragmatic people, and popular interest in the symbol rather than the content of higher education suggests the mania of democratic Americans for honorifics, a passion which led them to bestow colonelcies on countless frontier tavernkeepers.

II

Nine colleges had been established in the colonies before the Revolution, six of them after 1740. Their tone was aristocratic rather than popular; they attracted the sons of the well-to-do and a smaller number of poorer students who planned to become lawyers, doctors, or clergymen. It was clear by 1787 that state and local pride and the rivalry of Protestant denominations were causing collegiate institutions to multiply at an accelerating rate, but it could not yet be predicted how the expansion of higher education would be organized and directed. The first colonial colleges—Harvard, William and Mary, and Yale—had been mixed institutions, both public and private in character, sustained and supervised by established churches, private donors, and colonial governments.[6] This was a source of strength in stable communities, where political, economic, and religious affairs were managed by an interlocking establishment. In the eighteenth century, however, as sectarian and political divisions undermined the unity and stability of older communities and institutions, schools of mixed character became centers of turbulent controversy. Though the intellectual objectives of colleges were poorly appreciated, the control of these institutions often became a subject of bitter dispute, reflecting the divisions of an expanding society.

In this light the failure of the national university project can be understood. Discussed at the Philadelphia Convention of 1787, where a number of delegates wished to include authorization for such an institution in the Constitution itself, it was endorsed by presidents from George Washington to John Quincy Adams. Persisting interest in a great federally supported university in the capital city reflected the aspirations of early republican statesmen, who conceived of it first of all as a symbol of union, like the flag or the national capital itself. Future American leaders, they hoped, might receive suitable

6 See Beverly McAnear, "College Founding in the American Colonies, 1745–1775," *The Mississippi Valley Historical Review,* XLII, June 1955, 24–44. The American colonial college was a reproduction of the English college, a relatively independent unit within the university. At Oxford and Cambridge, by the seventeenth century, the collegiate foundations, originally designed as residences for young scholars, had absorbed academic functions and overshadowed the parent universities, which continued primarily as degree-granting bodies. In America, however, the colleges themselves assumed the power to grant degrees. Another feature distinguishing them from their English prototypes, and one which was to be of great significance in the history of American higher education, was the pattern of lay control. Only in America was it necessary for academic affairs to be managed by outsiders.

training in their own country rather than in Europe, where they would be exposed to monarchical ideas. At the same time, by bringing together young men from the different states, a national university could prevent the rise of sectional jealousies. Joel Barlow's *Prospectus* of 1806, the most interesting description of such an institution, reflects the influence of educational reforms in revolutionary France: provision is made for technical schools as well as for the education of political leaders. Barlow also suggested that the institution should perform research (without compensation to its faculty!) and serve as a central library and museum, and as an agency for standardizing textbooks for schools throughout the country as well.[7]

Some of these proposals were prophetic. The Smithson bequest in the 1830's made possible a national museum. The United States Military Academy at West Point (1802), the principal American engineering school before 1860, comprised another element of the national university scheme. After the Civil War, Andrew Dickson White of Cornell and some of the more articulate members of the Johns Hopkins faculty proposed the training of statesmen as an important function of their universities. But popular support for the sort of institution envisaged by Benjamin Rush, George Washington, and Joel Barlow was not forthcoming. And Jacksonian hostility to elitism would have prevented a federal university from functioning as a significant national influence even if it had been established. After 1815, efforts to charter such a university met increasing opposition. Constitutional scruples were raised to block a national institution while independent colleges multiplied. A central university was as distasteful to many Americans as a national bank, and for similar reasons, which had little to do with its educational merits.

7 Joel Barlow, "Prospectus of a National Institution, To Be Established in the United States," January 24, 1806. For a reconstructed text, see G. Brown Goode, "The Origin of the National Scientific and Educational Institutions of the United States," in American Historical Association, *Annual Report for the Year 1889* (Washington, D. C.: Government Printing Office, 1890), pp. 132–146.

Perhaps the outstanding exemplar of the sectional re-
luctance to endorse a national university was Thomas
Jefferson. Jefferson was not dogmatically opposed to national educational planning. He collaborated with the
French *émigré,* DuPont de Nemours, whose tract on
National Education in the United States of America was
published in 1800, and as president, he recommended
Congressional consideration of educational policy and a
possible Constitutional amendment to authorize broader
federal activity in this field. But his first concern was always for his native state. When George Washington
urged endowment of a national university in the capital
city in 1795, Jefferson sought to persuade him that the
institution should be located near rather than within the
Federal District, in that state which would pledge the
most generous contributions toward its maintenance. For
a short time, it seemed to him that public interest in a
national institution might make possible the realization
of his lifelong desire to establish a University of Virginia.
This project, the chief preoccupation of his old age, had
its roots in a broader educational scheme he had sketched
as early as 1779. A statewide system of public primary
schools would furnish its best pupils to regional grammar
schools, and the outstanding graduates of these institutions were to receive university training for the professions or for a life of leisure and public service. Elitist
rather than equalitarian in its stress on competence and
recognition of individual differences, Jefferson's approach
was not popular, even during his lifetime; in the Jacksonian era many Americans would find it undemocratic.

Jefferson never succeeded in persuading Virginians to
accept his comprehensive public school system. Bills to
establish the elementary schools, which he regarded as its
most important feature, were twice rejected. His state
university, however, was eventually established. During
the Revolution he had proposed to secularize William
and Mary, broaden its curriculum, and strengthen public
control over its affairs. After 1814, he abandoned the idea
of reforming William and Mary and sought to build an
entirely new institution near his beloved Monticello. It

is notable that the University of Virginia, which embodied so much of Jefferson's idealism, was established
only after years of political maneuvering. To win support for a university at Charlottesville he advertised the
advantages of the site and silenced proponents of other
towns by methods which would be followed again and
again in intrastate struggles over institutional location.
To mollify the patrons of existing private institutions,
Jefferson suggested in 1824 that the endowment of William and Mary be parcelled out to several newer colleges,
if they would become preparatory schools for his university; throughout his life he believed that institutions
established in one age should be subject to modification
by later generations. And, finally, as he made clear in a
letter to James Madison, Jefferson insisted that "political
orthodoxy" be maintained at the University of Virginia
and that its professors teach the prevailing doctrines of
his Republican party.[8] Thus, Jefferson's contributions to
higher education reflected the methods and prejudices of
a practical politician as well as the ideals of a philosopher
of the Enlightenment.

From its inauguration in 1825, the University of Virginia was unique: in form a university of European proportions, with elective studies and special qualifications
for degrees, it permitted students to attend for a longer
or shorter term as their needs warranted. With these
peculiar features, it became involved in the educational
debate of the 1820's, though collegiate reform in the
North was less directly affected by Jefferson's university
than by experiments at Harvard, Amherst, and Union.
Since the supporting structure of public elementary
schools and grammar schools which Jefferson envisaged
was not established, his university, however advanced in
form, remained largely collegiate in function.

The average American was aware that college distinc-
tions lent prestige to families of established wealth or to

8 Herbert B. Adams, *Thomas Jefferson and the University of Virginia,* United States Bureau of Education, Circular of Information,
No. 1 (Washington, D.C.: Government Printing Office, 1888), pp.
137–139.

ambitious professional men. Occasionally he sought them
for his sons, that they might rise in the law or the ministry. Generally, however, he was suspicious of profes-
sionalism and hostile to those whose possessions were not
acquired by hard toil or shrewd speculation. He was far
more likely to be influenced by an inspired preacher or
self-trained journalist than by a college president or edu-
tional philosopher. His assumptions—earthy, equalitarian, severely pragmatic—were increasingly reflected in
educational debates after the Revolutionary generation
had passed from the scene. They were expressed with
colloquial vigor in a remarkable document prepared in
1798 by William Manning, a Jeffersonian farmer and
Revolutionary veteran of North Billerica, Massachusetts.
Education, Manning insisted, should be cheap and practical. Existing colleges he dismissed as institutions for a
parasitical professional class. District schools and fearless
independent newspapers were the institutions most
needed to remedy the political and social injustices of
the Federalist era.

The self-trained journalists in whom Manning placed
his faith were generally hostile to the intellectual aspirations of educators. Discussions of college affairs in the
press were frequently concerned with personalities, or
with religious and political issues, and contributed little
to educational progress. A Concord newspaper treatment
of the dispute that led to John Marshall's decision in the
case of *The Trustees of Dartmouth College* v. *William H.
Woodward* (1819) is illustrative; the controversy itself is
significant for the insight it provides into the social environment of the old-time college.

Dartmouth's founder, the Indian missionary Eleazar
Wheelock, had bequeathed the presidency of the college
to his strong-willed son, John. A bitter quarrel in the
Hanover church led the younger Wheelock to launch a
pamphlet attack on the college's trustees; by this means
he hoped to invite legislative interference in Dartmouth's
affairs in order to strengthen his position. In 1815, the
altercation was appropriated by Isaac Hill, ambitious
editor of the Concord *New Hampshire Patriot*. Ignoring

the fact that most of the parties to the original dispute were themselves Federalists, and that their theological differences were slight, he described for his readers an imaginary plot of Federalist politicians and orthodox Congregationalists, led by the anti-Wheelock trustees, to subvert religious and political liberty in New Hampshire. His partisan assaults revealed utter disdain for serious educational purposes.

The Jeffersonian Republicans won the governorship in the state election of 1816, in which the affairs of Dartmouth College were a central issue; New Hampshire Federalism never recovered from this defeat. Unlike Isaac Hill, William Plumer, the successful candidate, was a man of high principle. Proposing in June 1816 that the State of New Hampshire assume a role in the management of Dartmouth College, he expressed a widely accepted philosophy of the Revolutionary generation, which had seen attempts to turn Pennsylvania and Columbia into public institutions and to subject Harvard and Yale to a measure of state management in return for financial aid. His legislature responded by creating "Dartmouth University," with an enlarged governing board in which the original College trustees were outnumbered by additional members appointed by the state. While faculty and students, divided into College and University factions, managed to coexist despite comic-opera crises, the College trustees and their alumni supporters instituted legal action to recover their rights. Aided by the eloquence of Daniel Webster ("It is, Sir, as I have said, a small College. And yet, *there are those who love it!*"), they won their case in the United States Supreme Court. Chief Justice John Marshall ruled that the Dartmouth College charter, granted by George III in 1769, was a contract, protected by the Federal Constitution against alteration by the state.

Marshall's decision, so important as a protection for corporate business, was equally significant for higher education. Henceforth, private institutions were legally shielded against legislative attempts to reshape their charters. Advocates of state educational systems could no

longer hope to reconstruct existing foundations. Political
and journalistic interference with higher education was
not checked, however. Isaac Hill's contempt for learning
was echoed by many later editors, and Governor Plumer's
efforts, based on Jeffersonian principles, were superseded
by irresponsible Jacksonian assaults. The Dartmouth case
had in truth cleared the way for a wasteful overexpansion
of weak colleges in an era of increasing hostility to state-
supported secular universities; but for private institutions which hoped to attain distinction it would be a
bulwark against unfriendly public sentiment.

   Discussion of collegiate reform in the Northeast during
the 1820's ultimately proved to be of greater national
significance than the establishment of the University of
Virginia. In this debate the most prophetic figure was
George Ticknor (1791–1871), a wealthy Bostonian and
Dartmouth graduate, who was studying in Germany at
the time of the crisis in his Alma Mater's affairs. A cor-
respondent of Jefferson's on educational matters, Ticknor
was one of a group of young Americans, including Edward Everett and George Bancroft, who returned to New
England between 1815 and 1825, filled with enthusiasm
for European scholarship and the universities of the Old
World. Assuming the Smith professorship of the French
and Spanish Languages and Belles-Lettres at Harvard in
1819, Ticknor aspired to reorganize the country's oldest
university after the German model. The immediate task
in Cambridge was to restore morale following a student
rebellion in 1823. Anticipating later university development, however, Ticknor proposed to arrange existing
courses according to departments and to regroup pupils
on the basis of their abilities, while allowing the election
of studies and encouraging alumni and others who were
not degree candidates to enroll in courses of their choice.
Thus, his proposals forecast the evolution of American
colleges into universities by departmental accretion and
the development of specialized learning characteristic of
Harvard. However, he had only partial success in persuading faculty and Corporation to accept his reforms.
His assumption of a rising public interest in distinguished

scholarship was unrealistic, stemming more from his own tastes and the enthusiasms he shared with a small circle of comrades from his European tour and close acquaintances in Boston and Cambridge than from an accurate assessment of popular demand. The indifference of most Americans toward intellectual achievement was evident even in the wealthier circles of Boston.[9] Ticknor had chosen the career of gentleman scholar and could not command the authority of a college president or a revered patriot; his efforts at Harvard met stubborn resistance. In the 1820's, however, he influenced both Thomas Jefferson and Francis Wayland, and a half-century later Andrew Dickson White and Daniel Coit Gilman were successful in developing universities of Germanic comprehensiveness.

Meanwhile, other projects were tried. In 1827, the Amherst faculty established a "parallel" course, emphasizing English literature, modern languages, and the sciences as substitutes for the ancient languages. Union College offered an alternate scientific course after 1828. At the same time, the University of Vermont, under its Transcendentalist president, James Marsh, announced an extensive rearrangement of course offerings designed to permit free electives and departmental specialization. Vermont was more conservative than Union and Amherst, however, in refusing to grant the bachelor's degree to students who had not completed the full classical course.[10] These experiments were received with apathy

9 See Francis J. Grund, *Aristocracy in America* (New York: Harper & Brothers, 1959), Chapter 10.

10 *The Substance of Two Reports of the Faculty of Amherst College, to the Board of Trustees, with the Doings of the Board Thereon* (Amherst, Massachusetts: Carter and Adams, Printers, 1827), and *An Exposition of the System of Instruction and Discipline Pursued in the University of Vermont. By the Faculty* (2nd ed.; Burlington, Vermont: Chauncey Goodrich, 1831). Although published materials on the rationale of the scientific course at Union College are inadequate, Butts (*The College Charts Its Course*, p. 134) and Schmidt (*The Liberal Arts College*, p. 59) are in error when they state that the A.B. degree was not granted to students completing this alternate curriculum. "College Education," a review of the Amherst reports (*North American Review*, XXVIII, April 1829, 294–311), attributed

and, with the exception of Union's scientific course, were abandoned after brief trial. The "partial course," a mere caricature of Jefferson's and Ticknor's ideal of an open university, continued to be offered at many institutions but it was never popular and fitted poorly into the rigid framework of the college system.

Though the public failed to respond to the opportunities offered by reformers, conservative educators were aroused. Their answer to the call for change appeared in the famous report of the Yale faculty in 1828, a vindication of the residential college and of the prescribed classical and mathematical course, tied to a forthright statement of the moral and pedagogical objectives they were intended to achieve. The traditional curriculum was upheld as ideally suited to discipline the mental "faculties," such as reason, imagination, and memory, and as an indispensable prerequisite to all advanced education. Parental supervision of students in a monastic college was imperative, since most undergraduates were impressionable adolescents. While Jefferson, Ticknor, Marsh, and Eliphalet Nott of Union proposed innovations designed ultimately to change American colleges into universities, the Yale faculty warned that injudicious experiments might imperil the ability of existing institutions to perform vital services.

For decades after 1828 the Yale Report sustained traditionalists.[11] Its assumptions seemed to reflect a realistic

to Professor Alpheus S. Packard of Bowdoin College, stresses the importance of maintaining the integrity of existing degrees, as does the University of Vermont *Exposition.*

11 Its influence is especially notable in the writings of Frederick A. P. Barnard during his pre-Civil War career in Alabama and Mississippi, though Barnard was a critic of the residential college. See [Frederick A. P. Barnard and John W. Pratt,] *Report on a Proposition to Modify the Plan of Instruction at the University of Alabama, Made to the Faculty of the University* (New York: D. Appleton and Co., 1855); Frederick A. P. Barnard, *Letters on College Government, and the Evils Inseparable from the American College System in Its Present Form* (New York: D. Appleton & Co., 1855), *Improvements Practicable in American Colleges* (Hartford, Connecticut: F. C. Brownell, 1856), and *Letter to the Honorable, the Board of Trustees of the University of Mississippi* (Oxford, Mississippi: University of Mississippi, 1858).

appraisal of the role played by American colleges and of the expectations of the public. The proposals of Jefferson and Ticknor, on the other hand, had exalted European models and assumed a national need for learning and professional specialization which few Americans recognized. Meanwhile, as new colleges multiplied across the West and South, Yale and Princeton (another bastion of conservatism) remained the most influential of the eastern institutions. Harvard, condemned as aristocratic and Unitarian, continued to draw students from distant states, but it had many critics even within New England and few conscious imitators. In the aftermath of the Dartmouth decision the Jeffersonian ideal of the state university was subordinated to the expansion of sectarian colleges. The Yale faculty's emphasis on moral purpose accorded well with the denominational impulse, which provided the major energy for collegiate development between 1815 and 1860.

In these years it became clear that each major sect intended to sponsor at least one institution in every state. College promoters followed in the wake of townsite speculators and revivalists. Unlike the Congregationalists and Presbyterians, many pioneer Methodists and Baptists preferred an unschooled ministry, but they soon joined the other denominations in the strenuous competition. The result was a host of cheap colleges broadcast across the land, catering to the convenience of potential students, but contributing nothing to advance the quality of American education. Here was the collegiate system William Manning thought the country needed. To clerical and lay leaders of Protestant denominations, moreover, church colleges were vitally necessary to avoid the dangers of "godless" state universities and the imagined menace of Jesuit domination of western education.

Along with other aspects of national growth, educational expansion was curtailed in times of economic adversity. The 1840's were an especially difficult period. In the aftermath of the Panic of 1837, colleges, ministerial aid funds, and other philanthropies faced severe contraction. In this atmosphere the educational debate of the 1820's resumed, and the proposals of Nott, Ticknor, and the Amherst faculty were refurbished by a leading educator who had sympathized with their objectives from the beginning of his career. Francis Wayland (1796–1865), president of Brown University from 1827 to 1855, now at the peak of his influence, was in most respects in an extremely fortunate position: autocrat of a medium-sized private college, held in awe by his students, dominant though not domineering over faculty and Corporation associates. As the oldest Baptist college and one of the colonial nine, Brown enjoyed national esteem, which was enhanced by the success of Wayland's textbooks in ethics and economics. Its management had always been shared by the Baptists with three other denominations, and Wayland, reared in the atmosphere of Eliphalet Nott's Union College, was determined to keep it non-sectarian. He was, in fact, becoming increasingly alienated from Baptist educational philanthropies.

Brown received generous support, however, from the leading Providence merchants and industrialists with whom Wayland worked closely. But he had never shared their aristocratic educational philosophy. His world was ruled by the laws of a sovereign Creator, laws which, he believed, applied to the management of colleges as to every other human activity. He never wavered in his insistence on the primacy of religious and moral purpose, the uniqueness of the responsibilities confronting middle-class Americans, and the efficacy of dedicated individual effort in achieving any result which men might wish to accomplish. Every educational project he sketched embodied two fundamental objectives: thorough teaching, which he regarded as essential in any field, and broad utility, which required a curriculum suited to the largest possible constituency. His sympathies embraced every kind of school and college, public as well as private, and almost every curricular innovation discussed during his lifetime. He paid little attention, however, to the historical development of human institutions. Dedication to moral duty was Wayland's guiding principle, the inspiration for years of arduous labor, as well as the source, on occasion, of a stubborn inflexibility.

The 1840's were critical years at Brown. Increased enrollment before 1837 had led to an expansion of the faculty; but no additional endowment had been secured for its support, and student aid funds which had been available earlier were depleted. Wayland's authority was in no way threatened, and the university's Baptist supporters and mercantile patrons stood ready to contribute to its resources. Wayland, however, was more concerned with adhering to his principles than with assuring the institution's survival. He could not in good conscience seek new funds, for he accepted Adam Smith's view that endowed salaries and scholarships were morally wrong and injurious to educational quality. Smith's educational economics, which had also appealed to Thomas Jefferson and George Ticknor, influenced Wayland's thinking profoundly, for his basic concern was with moral issues rather than intellectual improvement, and he saw in classical economics a system of laws which paralleled and reinforced those of moral philosophy. If Brown University were to survive, Wayland believed, it should do so as a solvent enterprise: faculty salaries should depend primarily upon fees paid by students, and additional pupils should be attracted by applied science courses, an elective system, and alternative degrees. Starting with a devotion to moral purpose and integrity of principle as firm as that of President Jeremiah Day of Yale in 1828, Wayland arrived at exactly opposite conclusions concerning the American collegiate system. Features which seemed vitally important to the Yale faculty were to Wayland purely expedient, to be preserved, modified, or rejected on the basis of utility. During the 1840's he engaged in a contest of endurance with his Corporation associates; receiving little support for his ideas of curricular reform, he stubbornly resisted pressure to launch a public appeal for endowment. From this controversy emerged two important contributions to educational literature.

Wayland's uncompromising adherence to the principles in which he believed masked his basic diffidence. He never relished the role of controversialist, and from its tone one would hardly suspect that his *Thoughts on the Present Collegiate System in the United States* (1842) stemmed from the most serious dispute of his presidency. This little treatise is a mine of information about the deficiencies of the pre-Civil War college. Every section reflects Wayland's dedication to duty and his hatred of idleness and complacency in trustees, faculty, and students. Its omissions are equally significant, for they reflect weaknesses in his educational thought. Viewing the functions of a college too narrowly in terms of his own belief in the importance of individual effort and moral purpose, he said nothing about the inherent value of liberal learning. His tendency to evaluate educational efficiency in the language of political economy is striking.

The economic approach predominates in Wayland's *Report to the Corporation of Brown University* (1850). Nearing the end of his career, he had finally obtained a mandate to institute comprehensive reforms; his *Report* was a prospectus of plans for which the university sought public support. But he had never clarified his priorities, and now he sought to achieve all at once numerous objectives, some of which were incompatible: a classical curriculum with higher standards, courses in the applied sciences, new alternatives to the bachelor's degree and suitable arrangements for students who sought no degree at all, public lectures, the fee system of faculty salaries, an elective curriculum, a more efficient system of student discipline, and the abolition of the residential college. Here was an attempt to modify almost every feature of existing colleges, undertaken by an educator who had never valued adequately the role of institutions in human affairs.

Wayland's 1850 *Report* was far more influential than his 1842 essay, for it appeared just as collegiate reform was again being widely discussed. Unfortunately its major effects were destructive. It was an obvious weapon for critics of the classics and was also utilized in politically inspired movements demanding, in the name of "popular education," changes in the management of existing institutions. For the Dartmouth decision had by no means provided trustees and faculties with immunity from legislative interference. Wayland had agreed with George Ticknor that colleges which did not meet the specific educational needs of merchants and artisans might wither away. Ambitious politicians were ready in 1850 to turn a prediction by two educators into a platform for official action, and institutions as far apart as Harvard and the University of Alabama became the targets of assaults in which Wayland's philosophy was employed in an attempt to force curricular reforms and to challenge the authority of incumbent officers.[12] Though Wayland had condemned reforms undertaken in response to "the harsh growl of popular discontent" in 1842, eight years later he had produced a document better suited to rally dissatisfied and anti-intellectual elements of public opinion than to sustain his fellow educators in their efforts to improve existing institutions.

Wayland's most constructive critic, Henry Philip Tappan (1805–1881), was well equipped to perceive the weaknesses in the Brown president's proposals. Like Wayland, Tappan had been a pupil of Eliphalet Nott at Union College and had taught and written on philosophy, but

12 On the threat to the classics see the defense of Wayland's "new system" by Asa Mahan and subsequent discussion at American Association for the Advancement of Education, 1851, in *Proceedings of the First Session of the American Association for the Advancement of Education, Held at Cleveland, Ohio, August 19th, 20th, 21st, & 22d, A.D. 1851* (Philadelphia: E. C. & J. Biddle, 1852), pp. 40–81. For the assault on Harvard compare Massachusetts, General Court, House of Representatives, [Document] *No. 164* [April 1850], by George S. Boutwell, with [Jared Sparks,] *A Memorial Concerning the Recent History and the Constitutional Rights and Privileges of Harvard College; Presented by the President and Fellows to the Legislature, January 17, 1851* (Cambridge: Published by John Bartlett, 1851); the significance of this crisis is discussed in Samuel Eliot Morison, *Three Centuries of Harvard, 1636–1936* (Cambridge: Harvard University Press, 1936), pp. 286–293. Basil Manly, in *Report on Collegiate Education, Made to the Trustees of the University of Alabama, July, 1852* (Tuskaloosa, Alabama: Printed by M. D. J. Slade, 1852), defends the traditional collegiate system against legislative pressure for "popular" education and includes a detailed survey of the results of collegiate reform experiments throughout the country during the preceding quarter-century.

his tastes and values were utterly different from those of Wayland. In the course of his teaching career in New York City, he had become a devoted scholar, urbane and well read; he was strongly influenced by his European travels, especially by his friendship with the French educator and philosopher, Victor Cousin. Tappan, too, was dissatisfied with the traditional college extolled in the Yale Report. And while his educational views were no less comprehensive than Wayland's, their breadth stemmed from his untroubled acceptance of all aspects of human culture rather than from an uncritical utilitarianism. His curricular proposals were designed to provide vocational preparation as well as humane and aesthetic experiences. Most important of all, he was the first major university promoter since Jefferson to be concerned with the entire range of schools. Tappan thought in terms of an architectonic system of institutions, culminating in great universities, such as he had observed in Germany, whose comprehensiveness expressed the philosophic value of all knowledge. As president of the University of Michigan from 1852 to 1863, he was primarily an institution builder, and he adhered to his educational philosophy with a dedication that Francis Wayland showed only on moral issues. "The question in education, as in religion, is not what men desire, but what they need," he wrote on the eve of his presidency.[13]

Tappan's administration ended in bitterness, and his vision has received inadequate acclaim from educational historians. From the beginning his position at Michigan had been both promising and insecure. He had set forth his purposes a year before his inauguration in *University Education,* a treatise inspired partly by his hopes of establishing a great university in New York City. The prospect before him in the West seemed bright. The University of Michigan had profited from the leadership of outstanding figures of the territorial era, and John D. Pierce, first Superintendent of Public Instruction, a New Englander attracted to the Prussian educational system

13 *University Education* (New York: George P. Putnam, 1851), p. 61.

as described by Victor Cousin, had made vigorous efforts
after 1837 to prevent the state university from being undermined by denominational colleges.[14] Despite these
advantages, however, a recently settled western state was
scarcely the ideal environment in which to build a Euro-
pean-style university. "Michigan is not Prussia, and Ann
Arbor not Berlin," wrote the editor of the Detroit *Free
Press,* Tappan's bitterest newspaper critic. Other communities were hostile to the development of one strong
institution in Ann Arbor, and the religious sects demanded representation on the university's faculty, while
seeking at the same time to establish their own com-
peting colleges. The slavery controversy, the Know-Noth-
ing hysteria, and the fanaticism of temperance reformers
embittered the political atmosphere and adversely affected the university's prospects. For all his magnificent
vision and rhetoric, Tappan could not cope with these
forces; in fact, he fatally weakened his own position by
his grandeur and haughty disdain for his critics, his
European tastes, and his unwise involvement in faculty
feuds. Ultimately the opposition of sectarians, temperance societies, and vindictive Regents forced his dis-
missal. Significantly, he spent his remaining years in
European exile. "Tappan was the largest figure of a man
that ever appeared on the Michigan campus," James
Burrill Angell remarked to Tappan's biographer. "And
he was stung to death by gnats!"[15] Eight years after his
departure, Angell, a pupil of Francis Wayland, took up
Tappan's work, and in more propitious times made
Michigan the outstanding nineteenth-century state university. Meanwhile, Andrew Dickson White, who had

14 See *Report of the Superintendent of Public Instruction of the
State of Michigan; Made to the Legislature, January 5, 1837* (Detroit, Michigan: John S. Bagg, 1837), pp. 40–41; the idea there
intimated is expanded in Pierce's 1838 *Report* (Michigan, Senate,
No. 4 [1838]) in a section entitled "Charters for Private Colleges,"
which includes opinions requested by Pierce from Francis Wayland,
Edward Everett, Heman Humphrey, M. Brown, and C. P. McIlvaine
on the effects of the proliferation of institutions.

15 Charles M. Perry, *Henry Philip Tappan, Philosopher and University President* (Ann Arbor, Michigan: University of Michigan
Press, 1933), p. 274.

begun his academic career as a historian at Michigan, drew on Tappan's ideals as well as on his own analysis of Tappan's errors in laying his plans for Cornell University, the institution which, more than any other, embodied the constructive contributions of the pre-Civil War educational debates.[16]

Evidently the citizens of Michigan were not much more sympathetic to an educational philosopher and institution builder at mid-century than the American public had been to the schemes of the Founding Fathers. But if Tappan's scholarly idealism could not stir men deeply, others hoped that a more pragmatic approach could. Around 1850, Harvard and Yale began to offer training in the applied sciences, though the Lawrence and Sheffield schools were kept separate from the liberal arts colleges; Wayland and Tappan both included engineering and agriculture in their plans for curricular development. But enthusiasts for "practical" education remained dissatisfied with the efforts of the older colleges, which had merely "hauled a canoe alongside of their huge professional steamships." Increasingly they advocated the establishment of distinctive new institutions whose chief purpose would be to provide training for young men destined for the "active professions." During the 1850's a vigorous debate between defenders of the liberal arts and the supporters of "people's colleges" was added to the still bitter controversies between sectarians and the advocates of public institutions.

Among the chief protagonists of agricultural and mechanical education were such figures as Horace Greeley, Jonathan Baldwin Turner, and Representative Justin Smith Morrill of Vermont. Morrill has won immortality for his landmark legislative contribution of 1862, but

16 [Andrew D. White,] *Report of the Committee on Organization, Presented to the Trustees of the Cornell University, October 21st, 1866* (Albany, New York: C. Van Benthuysen & Sons, 1867) sketches the structure and objectives of Cornell as it opened. For background see Walter P. Rogers, *Andrew D. White and the Modern University* (Ithaca, New York: Cornell University Press, 1942) and Carl L. Becker's witty and charming lectures, *Cornell University: Founders and the Founding* (Ithaca, New York: Cornell University Press, 1943).

neither he nor Turner nor any other single individual can properly be called the "father" of the land-grant college. The promoters of such institutions started with an assumption which the aristocratic Jefferson had shared with the Massachusetts farmer William Manning: that the laboring classes and the learned professions were two distinct groups in American society. Tappan's humane philosophy offered one means of bridging the gap between them, but its severe intellectualism had little appeal in a materialistic democracy. The Jacksonian influence precluded a return to the Jeffersonian ideal of trained elites, but the new concern for a broad range of vocational courses recalled the practical spirit of outstanding educators of the Revolutionary era. The advocates of industrial education in the 1850's anticipated the day when members of the learned professions would no longer comprise an educational aristocracy because a multitude of callings, on the farm and in the factory and office, would have been professionalized, and each provided with a suitable program of advanced education. Then, perhaps, the average American, who scorned foreign languages and philosophy as impractical, would rush to enroll in "democracy's college." The modern "service-station" university is a monument to their democratic inspiration—or to their intellectual insensitivity.

These men, however, like their predecessors in other collegiate controversies, were a small band of prophets and pioneers rather than spokesmen for a genuinely popular movement. Long after 1862, most farmers viewed land-grant colleges with suspicion. The ingrained anti-intellectualism of the average American disappeared slowly even when he had finally been offered courses specifically tailored to his vocational aspirations. Passage of the Morrill Act in 1862 was hardly evidence of popular commitment to the improvement of higher education. The law was in truth more of a "land-grab act" than a land-grant college act, and was strongly supported by eastern states which stood to claim acreage in the West and opposed for this very reason in many of the pioneer constituencies which the new colleges were supposed to benefit.

III

From the national university project considered at the Constitutional Convention of 1787 to the Morrill Act, signed by Abraham Lincoln during the Civil War, developments in American higher education had been closely related to the major events and forces in the nation's political and social history. In 1865, the great universities of which earlier generations had dreamed were about to become a reality: at Harvard under Eliot, at Cornell under White, at Michigan under Angell, and at Johns Hopkins under Gilman. These leaders drew many of their ideas from the discussions of the previous decades, and through their success they gained commanding influence and introduced a new era in the nation's intellectual development.[17]

Today, a century after the Morrill Act, American higher education faces an unprecedented demand for its services. A flood of students threatens to overwhelm existing facilities, and qualified applicants besiege every reputable institution. How are our colleges to meet the needs of greater numbers of students while improving the quality of their offerings?

The extraordinary influence of a few renowned schools is unmistakable. Historical forces have produced several national institutions to fill the role assigned by the Founding Fathers to a single federal establishment. The diverse character of leading American colleges and universities is a constructive legacy from the early academic promoters, while once-bitter controversies often seem remote and quaintly amusing. Current issues in higher education are usually more subtle in their complexity,

17 The impact of the age of the university on an institution that remained collegiate in character is treated perceptively in Thomas Le Duc, *Piety and Intellect at Amherst College, 1865–1912* (New York: Columbia University Press, 1946).

lacking the drama of a Dartmouth College case or the emotional fervor of a crusade for the "promotion of collegiate education at the West."

Though the specter of bankruptcy which haunted nineteenth-century educators has vanished, it has been replaced by the peculiar perplexities of an affluent age. Foundation subsidies, corporation gifts, and alumni contributions may permit well-established independent institutions to improve their standing, but it is significant that only one new institution of first rank, Brandeis University, has been created by private effort in recent years. Meanwhile, public appropriations have built an Air Force Academy and developed entire new state university campuses in such commonwealths as California. The weaker independent colleges face a precarious future, and the choices made by the stronger ones will be watched carefully. Oberlin, Reed, and Swarthmore have shown that the college may still be a vital institution, and Brown and Dartmouth have suggested that the collegiate atmosphere may be enriched by graduate and professional programs of high quality and restricted enrollment. The "university college" is likely to commend itself to other schools in a position to pursue a comparable course of development. Their experiments will be significant, for the continued vitality of private colleges is a matter of national interest.

The crucial problems of American higher education in the mid-twentieth century, however, must be confronted in a radically different environment. Today, as never before, the sprawling public university overshadows the small independent college. How many of them, one wonders, can ever be what the old-time college was at its best: an institution human in scale and humane in spirit? Contemporary universities have achieved many of the objectives of Jefferson, Wayland, Tappan, and Turner, but they are not precisely the institutions that any of these leaders would have designed. Their massive structures and diffuse objectives conceal conflicts of value and purpose which the ante-bellum debates never fully resolved. The pragmatic compromises which made modern American universities possible have not lessened the pertinence of major questions discussed before the Civil War.

Certainly the wisdom of the Founding Fathers' insistence on the nation's need for educational institutions of the highest quality is increasingly appreciated, but it is doubtful that genuine sympathy for Jefferson's goal of a democratically selected intellectual elite is widespread. Millions of Americans, intent upon material success or social status, have little understanding of the life of the mind and would be unprepared to face the full costs and consequences of equal educational opportunity, were the latter fully achieved. We still stand in need of forthright spokesmen to explain the nature and purpose of higher learning. Significantly, the most provocative recent analysis of national educational objectives has reformulated in contemporary terms a central issue on which the statesmen of the early republic differed from the Jacksonians: "Can we be equal and excellent too?"[18] There is no easy solution to this basic dilemma of our society.

Almost certainly, any answer which ignores our democratic traditions will prove unworkable. An a priori or purely philosophical reconstruction of the American university has never been possible, though in recent decades vigorous critics have implied that it should be attempted. Henry Philip Tappan understood this and was not ashamed to defend his ideal university in utilitarian terms. Crusades to democratize higher education, however, have often been marked by anti-intellectual implications. Few of Tappan's contemporaries shared the philosophical outlook on which he based his career as an institution builder. Francis Wayland's reform program had an ethical rather than a scholarly foundation; essentially he sought equal opportunity for all citizens to

18 John W. Gardner, *Excellence: Can We Be Equal and Excellent Too?* (New York: Harper & Brothers, 1961), and *The Pursuit of Excellence: Education and the Future of America,* Rockefeller Brothers Fund, America at Mid-Century Series, Special Studies Project, Panel Report No. 5 (Garden City, New York: Doubleday & Company, 1958).

obtain whatever training might be usefully applied for material success or moral improvement. But while Wayland was in no sense a crass vocationalist, his arguments, and those of the lobbyists for agricultural and mechanical education who followed him, encouraged the proliferation of vocational training courses, which in many universities have eclipsed the liberal arts, particularly the humanities. Our current concern with "excellence" may or may not stimulate a searching debate on these issues raised a decade before the Civil War. Should American colleges be based on Tappan's faith in the humane values of liberal education and the philosophical unity of all knowledge, or on Wayland's and Turner's desire to expand opportunities for practical training? Has the love of wisdom ever been the guide of life for many Americans? The answer may be discouraging to philosophers, but it would be heartening if more educators, particularly in public institutions, proclaimed objectives as broadly liberal as Tappan's, and with comparable courage and eloquence.

Though the curricular expansion for which reformers contended in the 1850's has been achieved in modern colleges, another element of the democratic faith may be in jeopardy. Educational costs continue to rise, and the tradition of free instruction in public institutions is practically dead (the undergraduate facilities of the City University of New York are a notable exception to this). Francis Wayland's desire that students bear the major burden of faculty remuneration may soon be realized, but poorer students, for whose sake nineteenth-century colleges maintained low fees, are already facing increasing difficulties. College expenses, it is said, should be regarded as a major personal investment, to be paid for on long-term credit. However reasonable this may appear in a society accustomed to installment buying, it is likely to restrict the opportunities for many capable students to obtain graduate or professional education, which is increasingly necessary for individual advancement and vital for national development. Fundamentally, as the founders of early state universities believed, the expan-

sion of educational opportunity is likely to depend more
upon public than upon private investment.

For this and other reasons the future development of
American higher education will be determined in large
measure by pressures of the voting and taxpaying public
on state and federal governments. More attention might
profitably be paid to the development of means by which
public support could be linked with private control, such
as the arrangements of the mixed institutions of the
colonial period, Andrew Dickson White's scheme for
Cornell to combine Morrill Act funds with private endowment and administration, or the British system
whereby Oxford and Cambridge receive large appropriations without formally becoming "state" universities.
At present, however, the outlook for innovations of this
sort in the United States is not bright. Americans are
accustomed to separating too sharply the spheres of public and private enterprise, and in higher education this
tendency has been strengthened by such historic episodes
as the Dartmouth College case. In view of the dangers of
modern totalitarianism, this concern should not be dismissed lightly, but it has also been responsible for much
sterility in the current dialogue between "liberals" and
"conservatives." Not only are most citizens unaware of
the beneficial results which might flow from an imagina-
tively conceived and generously supported federal program to subsidize higher education; they are equally
ignorant of ominous portents which have already
emerged as American colleges become increasingly dependent upon national policy.

The GI Bill of the 1940's and the post-Sputnik grants
since 1957 have stimulated improvements in college facilities and have contributed to enlarging individual educational opportunity. They were not intended to be forthright contributions to the improvement of our collegiate
system, however, but as responses to dramatic postwar or
cold war problems. This is disquieting, not only as an
indication of widespread indifference to education, but
also, and more fundamentally, as evidence of an inescapa-
ble and ominous challenge to our institutions and way

of life. Since 1940, the requirements of national security
have compelled American universities to devote a major
share of their facilities to military research and to direct students into fields where critical shortages exist.
Conceivably, future crises may make such great demands
on our higher educational system that vital questions
concerning its relations to individual aspiration and the
spiritual and cultural needs of our civilization will receive inadequate attention. Meanwhile, the public may
become less willing to tolerate intellectual freedom. If
disputes over religious orthodoxy, slavery and abolition,
or temperance could gravely damage colleges a century
ago when Americans were largely unaware of their importance to the nation's future, the continuing interna-
tional tensions of our own time are also likely to produce
serious threats to academic independence. How will our
universities stand up in another McCarthy era, and how
many southern institutions will resist the pressures of
frightened citizens and cynical politicians who would
sacrifice them in the struggle against racial justice?

In the final analysis, our early educational literature
is likely to be of greatest value as a source of inspiration
to a generation which faces problems of unprecedented
complexity. Bureaucratic efficiency and skillful public
relations alone will never sustain the quality of American
universities. Educational leaders must play a conservative
role, in the best sense of that much-abused word, but the
historical record suggests that they may often make their
greatest contributions by forthright espousal of principles
essentially bolder than the impatient criticisms of their
antagonists. This is the lesson to be learned from such
men as Thomas Jefferson and Henry Philip Tappan. The
integrity and idealism of the greatest ante-bellum educators is needed today more than ever before. American
colleges are neither ivory towers nor luxurious resorts;
they stand perilously exposed to dangerous crosscurrents.
A century ago their defenders sought to transplant European institutions, to uphold pedagogical standards, and
to instill a love for learning in a materialistic society.
Today's challenge is far more difficult: to protect and

strengthen costly and sensitive institutions which must search for truth by asking disturbing questions about man, society, and the universe in an age destined for persistent crisis and insecurity.

Department of History
University of Denver
August 1962

1.   George Washington
on a National University*
(1795)

*In the following letter, written to the Commissioners of
the Federal District, President Washington supported the
establishment of a national university in the future capital city, and offered to donate canal stock, previously presented to him by the Commonwealth of Virginia in
recognition of his public services, toward its endowment.*

PHILADELPHIA, 28 January, 1795.

GENTLEMEN

A plan for the establishment of a university in the Federal City has frequently been the subject of conversation;
but, in what manner it is proposed to commence this important institution, on how extensive a scale, the means
by which it is to be effected, how it is to be supported, or
what progress is made in it, are matters altogether unknown to me.

It has always been a source of serious reflection and
sincere regret with me, that the youth of the United
States should be sent to foreign countries for the purpose of education. Although there are doubtless many,
under these circumstances, who escape the danger of con-

* Text from *Washington's Words on a National University, Old
South Leaflets,* Vol. IV, No. 76 (n.p. [Boston], n.d.), pp. 4–6. For fur-
ther information on the national university project consult Edgar B.
Wesley, *Proposed: The University of the United States* (Minneapolis:
University of Minnesota Press, 1936), and documentary selections in
G. Brown Goode, "The Origin of the National Scientific and Educa-
tional Institutions of the United States," in American Historical
Association, *Annual Report for the Year 1889* (Washington, D.C.:
Government Printing Office, 1890), pp. 53–161.

tracting principles unfavorable to republican government, yet we ought to deprecate the hazard attending ardent and susceptible minds, from being too strongly and too early prepossessed in favor of other political systems, before they are capable of appreciating their own.

For this reason I have greatly wished to see a plan adopted, by which the arts, sciences, and belles-lettres could be taught in their fullest extent, thereby embracing all the advantages of European tuition, with the means of acquiring the liberal knowledge, which is necessary to qualify our citizens for the exigencies of public as well as private life; and (which with me is a consideration of great magnitude) by assembling the youth from the different parts of this rising republic, contributing from their intercourse and interchange of information to the removal of prejudices, which might perhaps sometimes arise from local circumstances.

The Federal City, from its centrality and the advantages which in other respects it must have over any other place in the United States, ought to be preferred, as a proper site for such a university. And if a plan can be adopted upon a scale as extensive as I have described, and the execution of it should commence under favorable auspices in a reasonable time, with a fair prospect of success, I will grant in perpetuity fifty shares in the navigation of the Potomac River towards the endowment of it.

What annuity will arise from these fifty shares, when the navigation is in full operation, can at this time be only conjectured; and those who are acquainted with it can form as good a judgment as myself.

As the design of this university has assumed no form with which I am acquainted, and as I am equally ignorant who the persons are, who have taken or are disposed to take the maturing of the plan upon themselves, I have been at a loss to whom I should make this communication of my intentions. If the Commissioners of the Federal City have any particular agency in bringing the matter forward, then the information, which I now give to them, is in its proper course. If, on the other hand, they have no more to do in it than others, who may be desirous of seeing so important a measure carried into effect, they will be so good as to excuse my using them as the medium for disclosing these my intentions; because it appears necessary that the funds for the establishment and support of the institution should be known to the promoters of it; and I see no mode more eligible for announcing my purpose. For these reasons, I give you the trouble of this address, and the assurance of being, Gentlemen, &c.

2. Thomas Jefferson
on Higher Education in Virginia*
(1814)

Jefferson's well-known letter to Peter Carr indicates the practical bent of his broad intellectual interests and his belief that higher education should be provided for a qualified minority, democratically selected. It refers to his earlier proposals for educational reform in 1779 and marks the beginning of the strenuous efforts which culminated in the opening the University of Virginia in 1825.

A LETTER FROM THOMAS JEFFERSON
TO THE LATE PETER CARR,

ORIGINALLY PUBLISHED IN *The Enquirer.*

Monticello, September 7th, 1814.

Dear Sir,—On the subject of the academy or college proposed to be established in our neighborhood, I promised the trustees that I would prepare for them a plan,

* Text from [Nathaniel Francis Cabell, ed.] *Early History of the University of Virginia as Contained in the Letters of Thomas Jefferson and Joseph C. Cabell* (Richmond, Virginia: J. W. Randolph, 1856), pp. 384–390. For additional information, see Gordon C. Lee, ed., *Crusade Against Ignorance: Thomas Jefferson on Education,* Classics in Education, No. 6 (New York: Bureau of Publications, Teachers College, Columbia University, 1961); Roy J. Honeywell, *The Educational Work of Thomas Jefferson,* Harvard Studies in Education, Vol. XVI (Cambridge, Massachusetts: Harvard University Press, 1931); and Philip A. Bruce, *History of the University of Virginia, 1819–1919: The Lengthened Shadow of One Man,* 5 vols. (New York: The Macmillan Company, 1920–1922).

adapted, in the first instance, to our slender funds, but susceptible of being enlarged, either by their own growth or by accession from other quarters.

I have long entertained the hope that this, our native State, would take up the subject of education, and make an establishment, either with or without incorporation into that of William & Mary, where every branch of science, deemed useful at this day, should be taught in its highest degree. With this view, I have lost no occasion of making myself acquainted with the organization of the best seminaries in other countries, and with the opinions of the most enlightened individuals, on the subject of the sciences worthy of a place in such an institution. In order to prepare what I have promised our trustees, I have lately revised these several plans with attention; and I am struck with the diversity of arrangement observable in them—no two alike. Yet, I have no doubt that these several arrangements have been the subject of mature reflection, by wise and learned men, who, contemplating local circumstances, have adapted them to the condition of the section of society for which they have been framed. I am strengthened in this conclusion by an examination of each separately, and a conviction that no one of them, if adopted without change, would be suited to the circumstances and pursuit of our country. The example they have set, then, is authority for us to select from their different institutions the materials which are good *for us,* and, with them, to erect a structure, whose arrangement shall correspond with our own social condition, and shall admit of enlargement in proportion to the encouragement it may merit and receive. As I may not be able to attend the meetings of the trustees, I will make you the depository of my ideas on the subject, which may be corrected, as you proceed, by the better view of others, and adapted, from time to time, to the prospects which open upon us, and which cannot be specifically seen and provided for.

In the first place, we must ascertain with precision the object of our institution, by taking a survey of the general field of science, and marking out the portion we

mean to occupy at first, and the ultimate extension of
our views beyond that, should we be enabled to render
it, in the end, as comprehensive as we would wish.

1. ELEMENTARY SCHOOLS

It is highly interesting to our country, and it is the
duty of its functionaries, to provide that every citizen in
it should receive an education proportioned to the condition and pursuits of his life. The mass of our citizens
may be divided into two classes—the laboring and the
learned. The laboring will need the first grade of education to qualify them for their pursuits and duties; the
learned will need it as a foundation for further acquire-
ments. A plan was formerly proposed to the Legislature
of this State for laying off every county into hundreds or
wards of five or six miles square, within each of which
should be a school for the education of the children of
the ward, wherein they should receive three years' instruction gratis, in reading, writing, arithmetic, as far as
fractions, the roots and ratios, and geography. The Legislature, at one time, tried an ineffectual expedient for
introducing this plan, which having failed, it is hoped
they will some day resume it in a more promising form.

2. GENERAL SCHOOLS

At the discharging of the pupils from the elementary
schools, the two classes separate—those destined for labor
will engage in the business of agriculture, or enter into
apprenticeships to such handicraft art as may be their
choice; their companions, destined to the pursuits of science, will proceed to the college, which will consist, 1st,
of General Schools; and 2d, of Professional Schools. The
General Schools will constitute the second grade of
education.

The learned class may still be subdivided into two sections; 1, Those who are destined for learned professions,
as a means of livelihood; and 2, The wealthy, who, pos-
sessing independent fortunes, may aspire to share in con-

ducting the affairs of the nation, or to live with usefulness and respect in the private ranks of life. Both of these sections will require instruction in all the higher branches of science; the wealthy to qualify them for either public or private life; the professional section will need those branches, especially, which are the basis of their future profession, and a general knowledge of the others, as auxiliary to that, and necessary to their standing and associating with the scientific class. All the branches, then, of useful science, ought to be taught in the general schools, to a competent extent, in the first instance. These sciences may be arranged into three departments, not rigorously scientific, indeed, but sufficiently so for our purposes. These are, I, Language; II, Mathematics; III, Philosophy.

I. *Language.* In the first department, I would arrange a distinct science. 1, Languages and History, ancient and modern; 2, Grammar; 3, Belles Lettres; 4, Rhetoric and Oratory; 5, A school for the deaf, dumb and blind. History is here associated with languages, not as a kindred subject, but on a principle of economy, because both may be attained by the same course of reading, if books are selected with that view.

II. *Mathematics.* In the department of mathematics, I should give place distinctly, 1, Mathematics pure; 2, Physico-Mathematics; 3, Physic; 4, Chemistry; 5, Natural History, *to wit:* Mineralogy; 6, Botany; and 7, Zoology; 8, Anatomy; 9, the Theory of Medicine.

III. *Philosophy.* In the Philosophical department, I should distinguish, 1, Ideology; 2, Ethics; 3, the Law of Nature and Nations; 4, Government; 5, Political Economy.

But, some of these terms being used by different writers, in different degrees of extension, I shall define exactly what I mean to comprehend in each of them.

I. 3. Within the term of Belles Lettres I include poetry and composition generally, and Criticism.

II. 1. I consider pure Mathematics as the science of, I, Numbers, and II, Measure in the abstract; that of numbers comprehending Arithmetic, Algebra and Fluxions;

that of Measure (under the general appellation of Geometry) comprehending Trigonometry, plane and spherical, conic sections, and transcendental curves.

II. 2. Physico-Mathematics treat of physical subjects by the aid of mathematical calculation. These are Mechanics, Statics, Hydrostatics, Hydrodynamics, Navigation, Astronomy, Geography, Optics, Pneumatics, Acoustics.

II. 3. Physics, or Natural Philosophy, (not entering the limits of Chemistry,) treat of natural substances, their properties, mutual relations and action. They particularly examine the subjects of motion, action, magnetism, electricity, galvanism, light, meteorology, with an &c. not easily enumerated. These definitions and specifications render immaterial the question whether I use the Generic terms in the exact degree of comprehension in which others use them; to be understood is all that is necessary to the present object.

3. PROFESSIONAL SCHOOLS

At the close of this course the students separate; the wealthy retiring, with a sufficient stock of knowledge, to improve themselves to any degree to which their views may lead them, and the professional section to the professional schools, constituting the third grade of education, and teaching the particular sciences which the individuals of this section mean to pursue, with more minuteness and detail than was within the scope of the general schools for the second grade of instruction. In these professional schools each science is to be taught in the highest degree it has yet attained. They are to be the

1st *Department,* the fine arts, to wit: Civil Architecture, Gardening, Painting, Sculpture, and the theory of Music; the

2d *Department,* Architecture, Military and Naval; Projectiles, Rural Economy, (comprehending Agriculture, Horticulture and Veterinary,) Technical Philosophy, the practice of Medicine, Materia Medica, Pharmacy and Surgery. In the

3d *Department,* Theology and Ecclesiastical History; Law, Municipal and Foreign.

To these professional schools will come those who separated at the close of their first elementary course, to wit:

The lawyer to the school of law.

The ecclesiastic to that of theology and ecclesiastical history.

The physician to those of the practice of medicine, materia medica, pharmacy and surgery.

The military man to that of military and naval architecture and projectiles.

The agricultor to that of rural economy.

The gentleman, the architect, the pleasure gardener, painter and musician to the school of fine arts.

And to that of technical philosophy will come the mariner, carpenter, ship-wright, pump maker, clock maker, machinist, optician, metallurgist, founder, cutler, druggist, brewer, vintner, distiller, dyer, painter, bleecher, soap maker, tanner, powder maker, salt maker, glass maker, to learn as much as shall be necessary to pursue their art understandingly, of the sciences of geometry, mechanics, statics, hydrostatics, hydraulics, hydrodynamics, navigation, astronomy, geography, optics, pneumatics, acoustics, physics, chemistry, natural history, botany, mineralogy and pharmacy.

The school of technical philosophy will differ essentially in its functions from the other professional schools. The others are instituted to ramify and dilate the particular sciences taught in the schools of the second grade on a general scale only. The technical school is to abridge those which were taught there too much *in extenso* for the limited wants of the artificer or practical man. These artificers must be grouped together, according to the particular branch of science in which they need elementary and practical instruction; and a special lecture or lectures should be prepared for each group—and these lectures should be given in the evening, so as not to interrupt the labors of the day. The school, particularly, should be maintained wholly at the public expense, on the same principles with that of the ward schools. Through the whole of the collegiate course, at the hours of recreation on certain days, all the students should be taught the manual exercise, military evolutions and manœuvres, should be under a standing organization as a military corps, and with proper officers to train and command them. . . .

On this survey of the field of science, I recur to the question, what portion of it we mark out for the occupation of our institution? With the first grade of education we shall have nothing to do. The sciences of the second grade are our first object; and, to adapt them to our slender beginnings, we must separate them into groups, comprehending many sciences each, and greatly more, in the first instance, than ought to be imposed on, or can be competently conducted by a single professor permanently. They must be subdivided from time to time, as our means increase, until each professor shall have no more under his care than he can attend to with advantage to his pupils and ease to himself. In the further advance of our resources, the professional schools must be introduced, and professorships established for them also. For the present, we may group the sciences into professorships, as follows, subject, however, to be changed, according to the qualifications of the persons we may be able to engage.

I. Professorship.
Language and History, ancient and modern.
Belles Lettres, Rhetoric and Oratory.

II. Professorship.
Mathematics pure—Physico-Mathematics.
Physics—Anatomy—Medicine—Theory.

III. Professorship.
Chemistry—Zoology—Botany—Mineralogy.

IV. Professorship.
Philosophy.

The organization of the branch of the institution which respects its government, police and economy, depending on principles which have no affinity with those of its institution, may be the subject of separate and subsequent consideration.

With this tribute of duty to the Board of Trustees, accept the assurance of my great esteem and consideration.

TH: JEFFERSON.

3.   William B. Rogers
on the University of Virginia*
(1845)

*The distinctive features of Jefferson's university are here
described in a legislative report of 1845. Many of its difficulties resembled those of other colleges, particularly
in the South; despite Jefferson's aspirations to create a
true university, his institution was essentially collegiate
in atmosphere. This report was prepared by William B.
Rogers (1804–1882), Professor of Natural Philosophy at
the University of Virginia from 1835 to 1853, and first
president of the Massachusetts Institute of Technology
(1862–1870 and 1878–1881).*

SYSTEM OF INTELLECTUAL CULTURE

On comparing the system of intellectual culture adopted
in this institution with that in use in the higher seminaries of learning in other states, we remark two distinctive features which from their influence upon the interests
of education, may be deemed worthy of especial note.
The *first* is the privilege allowed to students of selecting
such studies as have a more immediate reference to the
pursuits in which they design afterwards to engage, and

* *Report from the Committee of Schools and Colleges, Against the
Expediency of Withdrawing the Fifteen Thousand Dollars Annuity
from the University* [Virginia, House of Delegates], *Doc. No. 41*
[1845], pp. 2–3, 5–6. On Rogers, see *The Life and Letters of William
Barton Rogers, Edited by His Wife;* 2 vols. (Boston: Houghton,
Mifflin and Company, 1896).

the *second,* the practice of combining to an unusual extent oral instruction in the form of Lectures, with the use of text books.

It should here be added that many years before the establishment of the university the privilege of an election of studies was allowed at William & Mary. Within her venerable precincts liberal methods of instruction found a home long before they were adopted by the thronged and applauded colleges of New England; and in her halls were delivered by bishop Madison the first *regular* courses of lectures on physical science and political economy, ever given in the United States.

Election of Studies: The former of these peculiarities of system originating in a wise regard to the practical wants of society, has been found well adapted to the genius of our country, and at the same time eminently favourable to that thoroughness of knowledge which in a just plan of education is even more important than variety of attainment. In virtue of this system the student preparing for divinity, law, or medicine, is enabled to secure substantial attainments in ethics, metaphysics, and political economy, or in chemistry and general physics; the young engineer, in mathematics, mechanics and geology; and the incipient teacher, in the languages, mathematics, belles lettres and such other portions of knowledge as will accomplish him for his intended pursuits; while in neither case is he required to spend his resources and his time in the acquirement of branches which are but slightly related to the objects he has in view.

Nor does the privilege thus granted often lead, on the part of those who aim at a general education, to a neglect of the more difficult but yet indispensable branches of study, since custom has established a particular order of studies to which, with some modifications, the great majority conform. Besides, all are aware that, although a separate diploma is conferred in each department, nothing short of a full and thorough course in all the academic schools can prepare the student for the highest honours to which he may aspire.

It is not unworthy of remark that the advantages of such an election of studies, clearly evinced in the experience of the university, have been substantially recognized of late by the adoption at Harvard, and we believe other prominent institutions abroad, of a similar feature, to replace the Procrustes system hitherto in general use. But we may be allowed to add, that, while engrafting upon their old established methods this liberal improvement, they have allowed much *latitude* of election even to *their candidates for the higher honours,* and thus departing from the stern requisitions of our university, have held out inducements to the student to choose his studies rather in accordance with his fancy or love of ease, than with the claims of a rigorous mental discipline and a more profound and thorough scholarship.

Instruction by lectures along with text books: Adverting now to the other distinctive feature in the system of the university, the extensive use of lectures as a means of training and instruction, we would in the first place call attention to the fact that distinguished scholars abroad agree in regarding this mode of teaching as the most valuable improvement in the plan of university instruction witnessed in modern times, and that they ascribe to its inciting influences, both upon teachers and their pupils, much of that marvellous advancement in letters and science which has made so many of the seats of learning of the old world the renowned centres of a knowledge no less beneficent than bright.

The advantages of an extensive use of this method in association with text books, as compared with the old and still very usual practice of exclusive text book study and recitation, although as yet but imperfectly recognized in many of the colleges in this country, must, we think, become apparent from considering *first, the greater impressiveness* of knowledge *orally* conveyed, and *secondly,* the *more wholesome discipline* of the faculties which such a method renders habitual.

Respecting the former of these considerations it may be enough to add that this greater force and permanency of the impressions made upon the mind by the teachings of the lecturer, proceeding from a very simple law of our mental organization, is exemplified by the familiar experience of all, as well in the lessons imparted to infancy by maternal lips as in the oral instructions descending from the forum, the pulpit and the bar. In proof of the prevailing conviction on this subject in Europe as well as at home, reference might be made to the eagerness with which crowds of all classes of society gather around the desk of the distinguished expounder of philosophy, science or taste, and the earnest activity of thought with which they analyse and assimilate the knowledge he imparts. Indeed, so highly is this method of teaching valued at the present day, that while it has been made a prominent feature in the system of all the most active and successful institutions of learning in the old world, and has been *legitimately* applied as a most efficient mean of popular instruction by the learned and wise, it has not unfrequently been *spuriously* employed to deceive the simple and to tax the purses and the credulity of the uninformed. . . .

NUMERICAL SUCCESS OF THE UNIVERSITY

But while as we have seen the great objects of the founders of the university have been fulfilled so far as the method and extent of its instructions are concerned, it cannot be disguised that in another respect their hopes have been less fully realized. In the number of the students annually frequenting its halls, their sanguine calculations are found to have outstripped the progress of the institution. Yet it should here be remarked "that the number of individuals who receive at the University of Virginia the benefits of a collegiate education, is far greater than could be inferred from a comparison with the numbers of other similar institutions in other parts of the Union, since in these, in consequence of that gradation of classes through which every student is required to pass, most students continue at college four years; whereas under the system pursued here of allowing the student to attend such schools only as he selects, and to give his undivided attention to them, he obtains the honours of which he is most ambitious in a much shorter time. It would seem from comparing the whole number of students at the university in the last ten years, (1182,) with the number of matriculations in the same time, 2058, that the average term of their continuance is less than two years. In this way the number educated here may be equal to the number educated in colleges whose average annual number of students may be twice as great. The number of new students annually received at the university has in ten years averaged 118, and it is believed that there are not two colleges or universities in the Union, which have, on an average, received a greater number."

But while it would thus appear that the university even in this point of view has been far more successful than is often imagined, various influences have co-operated in debarring it from that great numerical prosperity which seems to have warmed the anticipations of its founders.

Injurious impressions as to the irreligious tendencies of the institution.—Among the causes of this shortcoming, especially in the earlier years of its history, we may in the first place mention the opinion very prevalent at the time, that irreligious influences were permitted and even exerted within its walls. An opinion which, though we are happy to say now very generally abandoned, is still found casting a shade of prejudice over the feelings of a few. Without entering into any enquiry as to the foundation of this impression as prevailing in former years, it is not inappropriate here to state, that no shadow of a pretext now exists, or has for many years existed, favourable to such a suspicion. We speak on the authority of the numerous pious divines of our own state and from abroad, who have either officiated as chaplains at the university or have otherwise become familiar with its internal influences and usages, when we assert, that in no similar institution in this country, is there a greater degree of respect voluntarily accorded to the ministers and ordinances of christianity, and in few are more numerous instances to be found of devout piety as well among the students as the professors and their families.

In further proof of the prevailing disposition on this subject at the university, we may point to the fact that the chaplain, *appointed annually from among the leading denominations in our state,* is supported exclusively by the *voluntary contributions* of the professors and other officers and of the students, and that through the same means a Bible society and Sunday school have long been in useful operation. It is but proper in this place to add, that while enjoying these high religious opportunities, the university, by the annual succession of chaplains of different denominations, is secured from that sectarian influence which in any other arrangement could not fail to impair its usefulness as a *state institution.*

Defective discipline in the early years of the University: Another obstacle to the numerical success of the institution, perhaps more influential even than that just stated, has arisen from the errors of discipline committed in the early period of its history. In an enterprise so novel in many of its features, it is not surprising that the scheme of organization however good throughout in theory should in some of its details have proved vicious or inadequate in practice. During this *experimental stage* of its career, it is well known that habits of dissipation and extravagance, with other offensive irregularities, prevailed among the students to a lamentable extent. The unfavourable impression thus occasioned in the public mind, far outlasting any reasonable cause in the government of the university, has continued, though with greatly diminished force, to obstruct its advancement even to the present day. The tragical occurrence which several years ago deprived the institution of one of its noblest ornaments, in the person of the learned and pious Professor Davis,* though solely chargeable to the unprovoked and reckless passions of a single youth, and entirely unconnected with considerations bearing upon the general discipline, was but too well calculated to extend the yet remaining prejudices caused by its earlier

* Murdered by a student in 1840.—T.R.C.

career. Yet it is pleasing to reflect that in spite of this terrible blow, from which not a few predicted that it would never be able to recover, and notwithstanding the depressing effects of the times, felt in our literary institutions as well as elsewhere, its career has since been marked by a steady increase in the number of its students. About 200 youths are now prosecuting their studies in the university, comprising in the academic courses, we believe, about one half of the entire number of young Virginians at present occupied in such pursuits, so that, should no untoward interference cripple its powers, we are justified in expecting within the next few years a larger class than has ever yet been gathered in its halls.

As respects the efficient character of its discipline, as now enforced, and the general absence of college vices and irregularities, we are fully authorized in saying that the university is most favourably distinguished in comparison with similar institutions abroad; while we may add, that the general excellence of its regulations is in nothing more strongly marked than in the earnest activity of a large portion of the students in their literary tasks.

Inadequate preparatory training: Along with the adverse influences above referred to, we should not neglect another whose effects in a great degree beyond the control of the institution, though gradually diminishing, must continue for some time to restrain its numbers and its usefulness. We allude to the defective *preparatory training* of by far the greater number of the youth educated at the ordinary academies and schools in Virginia and the more southern states. This lamentable defect, operating as a check upon the laudable aspirations of many who under other circumstances would be eager to profit by the higher teachings of the university, turns them away from her halls to stifle their cravings at home, or to seek in some other scene more easy access to literary honour, or should they venture into her precincts, without great energy of purpose, sometimes so fills them with discouragement as to divert their ambition to unworthy or pernicious aims.

4.   A Massachusetts Farmer
on Learning and the Professions:
William Manning,
*The Key of Libberty**
(1798)

*A striking statement of the anti-intellectualism and dis-
trust of the learned professions which were characteristic
of most Americans in the early national period appears
in this essay by William Manning (1741–1814), a Revolutionary veteran of North Billerica, Massachusetts. Written as the protest of a dedicated Jeffersonian against
Federalist rule in state and nation, it was intended for
newspaper publication after being "drafted over & corrected by some Larned Republican." It first appeared in
print in 1922, when its significance was pointed out by
Samuel Eliot Morison.*

*To all the Republicans, Farmers, Mecanicks, and Labour-
ers In Amarica your Canded attention is Requested to
the Sentiments of a Labourer*

Learning & Knowledg is assential to the preservation

* William Manning, *The Key of Libberty. Shewing the Causes
why free government has Always Failed, and a Remidy against it.
Adresed to the Republicans, Farmers, Mechanicks, & Labourers In
the United States of Amarica. By a Labourer.* Finished February
20th, 1798. Reprinted from *William and Mary Quarterly*, 3rd Series,
XIII, January 1956, 211, 217–218, 220–222, 225–226, 230–232, by
permission of Samuel Eliot Morison and the Institute of Early
American History and Culture. See Professor Morison's revised introduction, *ibid.*, pp. 202–208.

*of Libberty & unless we have more of it amongue us we
Cannot Seporte our Libertyes Long.*

I am not a Man of Larning my selfe for I neaver had
the advantage of six months schooling in my life. I am
no travelor for I neaver was 50 Miles from whare I was
born in no direction, & I am no grate reader of antiant
history for I always followed hard labour for a living. But
I always thought it My duty to search into & see for my
selfe in all maters that consansed me as a member of
society, & when the war began betwen Brittan & Amarica
I was in the prime of Life & highly taken up with Liberty
& a free Government. I See almost the first blood that
was shed in Concord fite & scores of men dead, dying &
wounded in the Cause of Libberty, which caused serious
sencations in my mind.

But I beleived then & still believ it is a good cause
which we aught to defend to the very last, & I have bin
a Constant Reader of publick Newspapers & closely
attended to men & measures ever sence, through the war,
through the operation of paper money, framing Constitutions, makeing & constructing Laws, & seeing what selfish
& contracted ideayes of interests would influence the best
picked men & bodyes of men.

I have often thought it was imposable ever to seport
a free Government, but firmly believing it to be the best
sort & the ondly one approved off by heaven it was my
unweryed study & prayers to the almighty for many years
to find out the real cause & a remidy and I have for many
years bin satisfyed in my own mind what the causes are
& what would in a grate measure prove a reamidy provided it was carried into efect. . . .

The soul end of Government is the protection of Life,
Liberty & property. The poor mans shilling aught to be
as much the care of government as the rich mans pound.
Every person in the Nation aught to be compeled to do
justis & have it dun to him promptly & without delay. All
taxes for the seport of government aught to be layed
equilly according to the property each person purseses &
the advantages he receives from it, and the peopel aught
to seport just so many persons in office as is absolutely

nesecary and no more, & pay them just so much saleryes
as will command sefitiant abilityes, & no more.

Also in free Government the most sacred regard must
be paid to the Constitutions established by the peopel to
gard their Rights. No law aught or can be made or constructed conterary to the true meening thereof without
becomeing a nullity & those becomeing gilty who does
it, let them be either Lejeslative Juditial or Executive
officers or bodyes of men. And no parte of the Constitution can be constructed conterary to the declared Rights
of the people.

In short a free Government is one In which all the
laws are made judged & executed according to the will &
interest of a majority of the hole peopel and not by the
craft cunning & arts of the few. To seport such a government it is absolutely nesecary to have a larger degree or
better meens of knowledge amongue the peopel than we
now have, which I shall indevor to make appear before
I close. . . .

In the swet of thy face shall thou git thy bread untill
thou return to the ground, is the erivarsable sentance of
Heaven on Man for his rebellion. To be sentanced to
hard Labour dureing life is very unplesent to humane
Nature. Their is a grate avartion to it purceivable in all
men—yet it is absolutely nesecary that a large majority of
the world should labour, or we could not subsist. For
Labour is the soul parrant of all property—the land
yealdeth nothing without it, & their is no food, clothing,
shelter, vessel, or any nesecary of life but what costs
Labour & is generally esteemed valuable according to the
Labour it costs. Therefore no person can posess property
without labouring, unless he git it by force or craft, fraud
or fortun out of the earnings of others.

But from the grate veriety of capacietyes strength &
abilityes of men, their always was, & always will be, a
very unequel distribution of property in the world. Many
are so rich that they can live without Labour. Also the
marchent, phisition, lawyer & divine, the philosipher and
school master, the Juditial & Executive Officers, & many
others who could honestly git a living without bodily

labours. As all these professions require a considerable expence of time & property to qualify themselves therefor, & as no person after this qualifying himselfe & making a pick on a profession by which he meens to live, can desire to have it dishonourable or unproductive, so all these professions naturally unite in their skems to make their callings as honourable & lucrative as possable. Also as ease & rest from Labour are reaconed amongue the greatest pleasurs of Life, pursued by all with the greatest avidity & when attained at once creates a sense of superiority & as pride & ostentation are natural to the humain harte, these ordirs of men generally asotiate together and look down with two much contempt on those that labour.

On the other hand the Labourer being contious that it is Labour that seports the hole, & that the more there is that live without Labour & the higher they live or the grater their salleryes & fees are, so much the harder he must work, or the shorter he must live, this makes the Labourer watch the other with a jelous eye & often has reason to complain of real impositions. . . .

The Reasons why a free government has always failed is from the unreasonable demands & desires of the few. They cant bare to be on a leavel with their fellow cretures, or submit to the determinations of a Lejeslature whare (as they call it) the Swinish Multitude are fairly represented, but sicken at the eydea, & are ever hankering & striving after Monerca or Aristocracy whare the people have nothing to do in maters of government but to seport the few in luxery & idleness.

For these & many other reasons a large majority of those that live without Labour are ever opposed to the prinsaples & operation of a free Government, & though the hole of them do not amount to one eighth part of the people, yet by their combinations, arts & skeems have always made out to destroy it soner or later, which I shall indeavour to prove by considering—

. . . .

ON THE IGNORANCE OF THE MANY

Solomon said, Train up a Child in the way he should go, & when he is old he will not depart from it. And it is as true that if a child is trained up in the way he should not go, when he is old he will keep to it. It is the universal custom & practis of monorcal & dispotick government to train up their subjects as much in ignorance as they can in matters of government, & to teach them to reverance & worship grate men in office, & to take for truth what ever they say without examining for themselves.

Consiquently when ever Revolutions are brought about & free governments established it is by the influence of a few leeding men, who after they have obtained their object (like other men) can neaver receiv compensation & honours anough from the people for their services, & the people being brought up from their uths to reverance & respect such men they go on old ways & neglect to search & see for themselves & take care of their own interists. Also being naturally very fond of being flattered, they redily hear to measures proposed by grate men who they are convinced have done them good services. This is the prinsaple ground on which the few work to Destroy a free government.

ON THE COMBINATIONS OF THE FEW

In a free government the few, finding their scheems & vues of interest borne down by the many, to gain the power they cant constitutionally obtain, Always indevour to git it by cunning & corruption, contious at the same time that userpation when once began the safty of the userper consists ondly in grasping the hole. To efect this no cost nor pains is spared, but they first unite their plans & scheems by asotiations, conventions, & coraspondances with each other. The Marchents asotiate by themselves, the Phitisians by themselves, The Ministers by themselves, the Juditial & Executive Officers are by their pro-

fessions often called together & know each others minds,
& all letirary men & the over grown rich, that can live
without labouring, can spare time for consultation. All
being bound together by common interest, which is the
stronges bond of union, join in their secret corraspond-
ance to counter act the interests of the many & pick their
pockets, which is efected ondly for want of the meens of
knowledg amongue them.

ON LARNING

Larning is of the gratest importance to the seport of
a free government, & to prevent this the few are always
crying up the advantages of costly collages, national
acadimyes & grammer schooles, in ordir to make places
for men to live without work, & so strengthen their party.
But are always opposed to cheep schools & woman schools,
the ondly or prinsaple means by which larning is spred
amongue the Many.

ON KNOWLEDGE

The gratest & best meens of obtaining the knowledge
nesecary for a free man to have, is by the Liberty of the
Press, or publick Newspapers. To counter act and destroy this priviledge the few spare no pains to make them
as costly as posable & to contradict everything in them
that favours the interests of the Many, puting Darkness
for Light, & Light for Darkness, falsehood for truth, &
truth for falsehood, &cc. . . .

ON DOCTORS

The Doctors have established their Meditial Societyes
& have both their State & County Meetings, by which they
have so nearly enielated Quacary of all kinds, that a poor
man cant git so grate cures of them now for a ginna, as
he could 50 years ago of an old Squaw for halfe a pint
of Rhum. The bisness of a Midwife could be purformed
50 years ago for halfe a doller & now it costs a poor man
5 hole ones. . . .

ON LITERARY MEN & COLEDGES

The true prinsaples of Republicanisam & a free government may be taught to the Uths in some of our Coleges & Acadimies for aught I know, but it is evident that other political prinsaples are admited in many of them, or we should not be stunded with Exhibitions in favour of Monocyes & runing down Republican prinsaples as we often be. One thing is prity cartain, that the Schollers are taught to keep up the dignity of their professions, for if we apply for a preacher or a School Master, we are told the price So Much, & they cant go under, for it is agreed upon & they shall be disgrased if they take less, let their abilityes for the servis be what they will. . . .

ON LAWYERS

The Lawyers have established their Bar Meetings & become the most formidable & influential ordir of any in the Government, & though they are nither Juditial nor Executive officers, but a kind of Mule ordir, ingendered by, & many times overawing both. This ordir of men git their living intirely from the quarrils follyes disputes & destreses of the Many & the intricacy of our Laws, & it is from the arts & doings of these men, that the Juditial & Executive officers are furnished with the chief of their bisness & imploy. Consiquently they are bound together by the strongest bonds of union. . . .

ON LARNING

No person who is a frind to Libberty will be against a large expence in Larning, but it aught to be promoted in the cheepest & best manner possable, which in my oppinnion would be:—For every State to maintain as many Coledges in conveniant parts thereof as would be attended upon to give the highest Degrees of Larning, & for every County to keep as many Grammer Schools or

Acadimics in conveniant parts thereof as would be attended too by both sects summer & winter, & no student or scholer to pay anything for tuition, and for the County Schooles to pay a purticuler attention to teaching the Inglish langueg & qualifying its scholors to teach & govern Common Schools for little children.

And for Every Town to be obliged to keep as Much as six weeks of wrighting school in the winter & twelve weeks of a woman school in the summer in every parte of the town. So that none should be thronged with two many schollers, nor none have too far to travel, & every person be obliged to send his children to school, for the publick are as much interested in the Larning of one child as an other.

If this method of Larning was established we should soone have a plenty of school masters & mistrises as cheep as we could hire other labour, & Labour & Larning would be conected together & lesen the number of those that live without work. Also we should have a plenty of men to fill the highest offices of State for less than halfe we now give. But insted of this mode of Larning the few are always striving to oblige us to maintain grait men with grate salleryes & to maintain Grammer Schools in every town to teach our Children a b c all which is ondly to give imploy to gentlemens sons & make places for men to live without worke. For their is no more need of a mans haveing a knowledge of all the languages to teach a Child to read write & cifer than their is for a farmer to have the marinors art to hold plow.

ON KNOWLIDGE

The prinsaple knowledge nesecary for a free man to have is obtained by the Libberty of the press or publick newspapers. But this kind of knowledge is almost ruened of late by the doings of the few. But a few years ago we could have the hole news by one paper in a week, & could put some dependance on what was printed. But the few, being closely combined & determined to destroy our Government, find it nesecary to destroy the Liberty of the press first. To efect this they imploy no printers, but those that will adhear strictly to their vuies & interests, & use all the arts & retrick hell can invent to blackgard the Republican printers & all they print, & strive to make the peopel believe falsehood for truts & truts for falsehood, & as they have money & lasure they have their papers every day in the week. Consiquently the Republican printers double their papers, so that a labouring man must now be at the expence of three or four dollers anually & read & studdy halfe his time, & then be at a loss to know what is true & what not—thus the few have almost ruened the Libberty of the press.

5. The Dartmouth College Case

Isaac Hill* (1815)

Isaac Hill's treatment of the affairs of Dartmouth College in the New Hampshire Patriot *in 1815 helped transform an academic controversy into a critical issue in state politics. His style and prejudices are typical of countless attacks on colleges by self-trained journalists of the nineteenth century. Hill's extensive political career included membership in Andrew Jackson's "Kitchen Cabinet."*

Who are the *excusers* of Dr. Wheelock? First, Isaac Hill, editor of the New-Hampshire Patriot, of whom it is necessary to say but little. With *us* his character is well known. *He probably never saw the inside of a College* &c. The *respectable* editor of the Boston Daily Advertiser, [yes, very respectable, and very learned, and very wise, no doubt, because he is not only a federalist, but has seen "the inside of a College"] probably knows as little of the concerns of Dartmouth College, as the aforesaid Isaac Hill, and his prejudices are quite as strong against it. These are the men that print the writings, &c.

—*Portsmouth Oracle*

True it is, that President WHEELOCK finds few of the federal papers willing to espouse his cause: the *leaders* of the federal party—those leaders who for years have combined to unite Church and State—to control public opinion by means of the influence of the federal Clergy —to "put down" every man who disputes their Sectarian creed, or their right to disfranchise all who will not combine in their unholy league;—these leaders at present have nearly every federal paper in New-England under

* *New Hampshire Patriot* (Concord), October 24, 1815. On Hill, see *Dictionary of American Biography*, Vol. IX, pp. 34–35.

their thumb. We are surprised that even the "respectable
editor of the Boston Daily Advertiser" should publish
communications which unfold their plots. The *Oracle* is
known to be directed by one of the *"Club,"* a very scientific, learned, "inside-of-a-College" man—who went
"through College," as they term it, by begging, and it is
said afterwards abused his benefactors—who professes to
be religious for the same reason that his *spectacled* master and "club" colleague professes to be religious, and
for the same reason that another conspicuous character,
also deep in their plot, sometimes *quotes scripture*—the
better to deceive—who makes long speeches in Congress,
and probably puffs them in the Oracle as "diamonds of
the first water." Hence it is not surprising that the
Oracle should join heart and hand "to put down"
President WHEELOCK.

We have always said, and we now repeat, that the
question agitated at Dartmouth College was a *political
question*. We know that very many respectable federalists are on the *republican side* of this question; we know
that thousands of federalists in New-Hampshire are dissatisfied with the conduct of the Conspirators leagued to
unite Church and State—and abhor the idea of com-
pelling people to subscribe to the dogmas of a sectarian
faction. President Wheelock is not the only victim
whose name is written in the book of proscription. Let
Doct. M'Farland* write till doomsday, protesting the
liberality of himself and colleagues—let him declare
there is no difference between Presbyterians and Congregationalists—that himself was once a Presbyterian and
that Dr. Phillips was a Congregationalist: we never can
believe that all Presbyterians are persecutors, or that all
Congregationalists are engaged, with the Theological
Seminary at Andover, in building up a sectarian party
that intends to "put down" all opposition: we never can
believe that President Wheelock did not incur the venge-
ance of this faction, and that his liberality towards all

* The Rev. Asa McFarland of Concord, whose election as a trustee
of Dartmouth College in 1809 had strengthened President Wheelock's
enemies, contributed to the attack on him in the press in 1815.
—T.R.C.

denominations was not the real source of the bitterness and persecution he has felt.

Without incurring the charge of egotism, the paragraph in the Oracle will justify us in saying a word of ourselves. "He ["Isaac Hill"] probably never saw the inside of a College"—as if it was a disgrace not to have the honors of a University. We might tell this writer that WASHINGTON had not a College education, and that FRANKLIN was once a humble printer like ourselves: perhaps either of these names will sound as well in future history as that of "Mr. D. W." * If, however, this does not satisfy the college-learnt scribbler in the *Oracle,* we will read to him a verse or two from our favorite bard, ROBERT BURNS, whose education was humble as our own, but whose name shall live when that of many "college dunces" shall be forgotten.

> What's all your jargon of your schools,
> Your Latin names for horns and stools;
> If honest nature made you *fools.*
>   What sairs your grammars?
> Ye'd better ta'en up spades and shools,
>   Or knappin-hammers.
>
> A set o' dull conceited hashes,
> Confuse their brains in college classes!
> They *gang in* stirks and *come out* asses,
>   Plain truth to speak;
> And syne they think to climb Parnassus
>   By dint o' Greek!
>
> Give me one spark o' Nature's fire,
> That's a' the learning I desire.* *

* Daniel Webster, who resided in Portsmouth, N.H., from 1807 until 1816, and was elected to Congress as a Federalist representative in 1813. He is also referred to in the first paragraph. From the beginning of his political career, Webster was subjected to bitter abuse by Hill, who considered the Portsmouth *Oracle* Webster's mouthpiece and condemned its "stupidity and malevolence." Ironically Webster's national fame as a brilliant lawyer and eloquent orator was first established by his successful defense of the Dartmouth College charter before the Supreme Court in 1818. See Claude Moore Fuess, *Daniel Webster* (Boston: Little, Brown and Company, 1930), I, 146, 215–245.—T.R.C.

* *"Epistle to J. Lapraik, An Old Scottish Bard, April 1, 1785." —T.R.C.

William Plumer* (1816)

A former Federalist converted to Jeffersonian Republicanism before the War of 1812, William Plumer won election as Governor of New Hampshire in 1816 as an advocate of state intervention in the affairs of Dartmouth College. In his message to the legislature, June 6, he requested alterations in the governing board established by the charter of 1769 which would guarantee public control of the institution. Plumer's principles had been widely accepted in the Revolutionary era. Thomas Jefferson wrote to him on July 21, 1816, praising the address: "The idea that institutions established for the use of the nation cannot be touched nor modified, even to make them answer their end, because of rights gratuitously supposed in those employed to manage them in trust for the public, may perhaps be a salutary provision against the abuses of a monarch, but is most absurd against the nation itself."

There is no system of government, where the general diffusion of knowledge is so necessary as in a Republic. It is therefore not less the duty than the interest of the State to patronize and support the cause of literature and the sciences. So sensible were our ancestors of this, that they early made provision for schools, academies and a college, the good effects of which we daily experience.

* *New Hampshire Patriot* (Concord), June 11, 1816. On Plumer, see *Dictionary of American Biography*, Vol. XV, pp. 12–13, and Lynn W. Turner, *William Plumer of New Hampshire, 1759–1850* (Chapel Hill: Published for the Institute of Early American History and Culture by the University of North Carolina Press, 1962). The roles of Plumer and Isaac Hill are contrasted in William Gwyer North, "The Political Background of the Dartmouth College Case," *New England Quarterly*, XVIII, June 1945, 181–203.

But all literary establishments, like every thing human, if not duly attended to, are subject to decay; permit me therefore to invite your consideration to the state and condition of Dartmouth college, the head of our learned institutions. As the State has contributed liberally to the establishment of its funds, and as our constituents have a deep interest in its prosperity, it has a strong claim to our attention. The charter of that college was granted December 30th, 1769, by John Wentworth, who was then governor of New Hampshire under the authority of the British king. As it emanated from royalty, it contained, as was natural it should, principles congenial to monarchy. Among others it established trustees, made seven a quorum, and authorized a majority of those present to remove any of its members which they might consider unfit or incapable, and the survivors *to perpetuate the board by themselves electing others to supply vacancies.* This last principle is hostile to the spirit and genius of a free government. Sound policy therefore requires that the mode of election should be changed, and that trustees in future should be elected by some other body of men. To increase the number of trustees, would not only increase the security of the college, but be a mean of interesting more men in its prosperity. If it should be made in future the duty of the President, annually in May, to report to the Governor a full and particular account of the state of the funds, their receipts and expenditures, the number of students and their progress, and generally the state and condition of the college, and the governor to communicate this statement to the legislature in their June session; this would form a check upon the proceedings of the trustees, excite a spirit of attention in the officers and students of the college, and give to the legislature such information as would enable them to act with greater propriety upon whatever may relate to that institution.

The college was formed for the public good, not for the benefit or emolument of its trustees; and the right to amend and improve acts of incorporation of this nature, has been exercised by all governments, both monarchical and republican. Sir Thomas Gresham established a fund to support lecturers in Gresham college in London, upon the express condition that the lecturers should be unmarried men, and upon their being married their interest in the fund should absolutely cease; but the British parliament in the year 1768, passed a law removing the college to another place, and explicitly enacted that if the lecturers were married, or should marry, they should receive their fees and stipend out of the fund, any restriction or limitation in the will of the said Gresham to the contrary notwithstanding. In this country a number of the States have passed laws that made material changes in the charters of their colleges. And in this State acts of incorporation of a similar nature have frequently been amended and changed by the legislature. By the several acts incorporating towns their limits were established; but whenever the legislature judged that the public good required a town to be made into two, they have made the division, and in some instances against the remonstrance of a majority of its inhabitants. In the charter of Dartmouth college it is expressly provided that the president, trustees, professors, tutors and other officers shall take the oath of allegiance to the British king; but if the laws of the United States, as well as those of New-Hampshire, abolished by implication that part of the charter, much more might they have done it directly and by express words. These facts shew the authority of the legislature to interfere upon this subject; and I trust you will make such further provisions as will render this important institution more useful to mankind. . . .

WILLIAM PLUMER.

State of New-Hampshire,
June 6, 1816.

John Marshall* (1819)

In a momentous decision for American constitutional law, Chief Justice John Marshall on February 2, 1819, sustained the Dartmouth charter of 1769 as a contract, protected by the Federal Constitution against alteration by the state, thus nullifying New Hampshire's efforts to remodel the college's governing board. Marshall's remarks on corporations are famous; his discussion of private philanthropy in education has been reprinted less frequently.

This is an action of trover, brought by the trustees of Dartmouth College against William H. Woodward, in the State Court of New Hampshire, for the book of records, corporate seal, and other corporate property, to which the plaintiffs allege themselves to be entitled. . . .

The title of the plaintiffs originates in a charter dated the 13th day of December, in the year 1769, incorporating twelve persons therein mentioned, by the name of "The Trustees of Dartmouth College," granting to them and their successors the usual corporate privileges and powers, and authorizing the trustees, who are to govern the college, to fill up all vacancies which may be created in their own body.

The defendant claims under three acts of the legislature of New Hampshire, the most material of which was

* *The Trustees of Dartmouth College* v. *Woodward*, 4 Wheaton 518; 4 Legal Ed. 629 (1819). For additional information, consult Leon B. Richardson, *History of Dartmouth College*, 2 vols. (Hanover, New Hampshire: Dartmouth College Publications, 1932); Albert J. Beveridge, *The Life of John Marshall* (Boston: Houghton Mifflin Company, 1919), Vol. IV, Chapter 5; and Charles Grove Haines, *The Role of the Supreme Court in American Government and Politics, 1789–1835* (Berkeley: University of California Press, 1944), Chapter 11.

passed on the 27th of June, 1816, and is entitled, "an act to amend the charter, and enlarge and improve the corporation of Dartmouth College." Among other alterations in the charter, this act increases the number of trustees to twenty-one, gives the appointment of the additional members to the executive of the state, and creates a board of overseers, with power to inspect and control the most important acts of the trustees. This board consists of twenty-five persons. The president of the senate, the speaker of the house of representatives, of New Hampshire, and the Governor and Lieutenant-Governor of Vermont, for the time being, are to be members *ex officio*. The board is to be completed by the Governor and council of New Hampshire, who are also empowered to fill all vacancies which may occur. The acts of the 18th and 26th of December are supplemental to that of the 27th of June, and are principally intended to carry that act into effect.

The majority of the trustees of the college have refused to accept this amended charter, and have brought this suit for the corporate property, which is in possession of a person holding by virtue of the acts which have been stated.

It can require no argument to prove that the circumstances of this case constitute a contract. An application is made to the crown for a charter to incorporate a religious and literary institution. In the application, it is stated that large contributions have been made for the object, which will be conferred on the corporation as soon as it shall be created. The charter is granted, and on its faith the property is conveyed. Surely in this transaction every ingredient of a complete and legitimate contract is to be found.

The points for consideration are:

1. Is this contract protected by the constitution of the United States?

2. Is it impaired by the acts under which the defendant holds? . . .

The parties in this case differ less on general principles, less on the true construction of the constitution in the abstract, than on the application of those principles to this case, and on the true construction of the charter of 1769. This is the point on which the cause essentially depends. If the act of incorporation be a grant of political power, if it create a civil institution to be employed in the administration of the government, or if the funds of the college be public property, or if the state of New Hampshire, as a government, be alone interested in its transactions, the subject is one in which the legislature of the state may act according to its own judgment, unrestrained by any limitation of its power imposed by the constitution of the United States.

But if this be a private eleemosynary institution, endowed with a capacity to take property for objects unconnected with government, whose funds are bestowed by individuals on the faith of the charter; if the donors have stipulated for the future disposition and management of those funds in the manner prescribed by themselves, there may be more difficulty in the case, although neither the persons who have made these stipulations nor those for whose benefit they were made, should be parties to the cause. Those who are no longer interested in the property, may yet retain such an interest in the preservation of their own arrangements as to have a right to insist that those arrangements shall be held sacred. Or, if they have themselves disappeared, it becomes a subject of serious and anxious inquiry, whether those whom they have legally empowered to represent them forever may not assert all the rights which they possessed, while in being; whether, if they be without personal representatives who may feel injured by a violation of the compact, the trustees be not so completely their representatives, in the eye of the law, as to stand in their place, not only as respects the government of the college, but also as respects the maintenance of the college charter. . . .

. . . Dartmouth College is really endowed by private individuals, who have bestowed their funds for the propogation of the Christian religion among the Indians, and for the promotion of piety and learning generally. From these funds the salaries of the tutors are drawn; and these salaries lessen the expense of education to the students. It is, then, an eleemosynary, and, as far as respects its funds, a private corporation.

Do its objects stamp on it a different character? Are the trustees and professors public officers, invested with any portion of political power, partaking in any degree in the administration of civil government, and performing duties which flow from the sovereign authority?

That education is an object of national concern, and a proper subject of legislation, all admit. That there may be an institution founded by government, and placed entirely under its immediate control, the officers of which would be public officers, amenable exclusively to government, none will deny. But is Dartmouth College such an institution? Is education altogether in the hands of government? Does every teacher of youth become a public officer, and do donations for the purpose of education necessarily become public property, so far that the will of the legislature, not the will of the donor, becomes the law of the donation? These questions are of serious moment to society, and deserve to be well considered.

Doctor [Eleazar] Wheelock, as the keeper of his charity-school, instructing the Indians in the art of reading, and in our holy religion; sustaining them at his own expense, and on the voluntary contributions of the charitable, could scarcely be considered as a public officer, exercising any portion of those duties which belong to government; nor could the legislature have supposed that his private funds, or those given by others, were subject to legislative management, because they were applied to the purposes of education. When, afterwards, his school was enlarged, and the liberal contributions made in England, and in America, enabled him to extend his cares to the education of the youth of his own country, no change was wrought in his own character, or in the nature of his duties. . . .

A corporation is an artificial being, invisible, intangible, and existing only in contemplation of law. Being the mere creature of law, it possesses only those properties which the charter of its creation confers upon it, either expressly or as incidental to its very existence. These are such as are supposed best calculated to effect the object for which it was created. Among the most important are immortality, and, if the expression may be allowed, individuality; properties by which a perpetual succession of many persons are considered as the same, and may act as a single individual. They enable a corporation to manage its own affairs, and to hold property without the perplexing intricacies, the hazardous and endless necessity, of perpetual conveyances for the purpose of transmitting it from hand to hand. It is chiefly for the purpose of clothing bodies of men, in succession, with these qualities and capacities, that corporations were invented, and are in use. By these means, a perpetual succession of individuals are capable of acting for the promotion of the particular object, like one immortal being. But this being does not share in the civil government of the country, unless that be the purpose for which it was created. Its immortality no more confers on it political power, or a political character, than immortality would confer such power or character on a natural person. It is no more a state instrument than a natural person exercising the same powers would be. If, then, a natural person, employed by individuals in the education of youth, or for the government of a seminary in which youth is educated, would not become a public officer, or be considered as a member of the civil government, how is it that this artificial being, created by law, for the purpose of being employed by the same individuals for the same purposes, should become a part of the civil government of the country? Is it because its existence, its capacities, its powers, are given by law? Because the government has given it the power to take and to hold property in a particular form, and for particular purposes, has the government a consequent right substantially to change that form, or to vary the purposes to which the property is to be applied? This principle has never been asserted or recognized, and is supported by no authority. Can it derive aid from reason?

The objects for which a corporation is created are

universally such as the government wishes to promote.
They are deemed beneficial to the country; and this
benefit constitutes the consideration, and, in most cases,
the sole consideration of the grant. In most eleemosynary
institutions, the object would be difficult, perhaps unat-
tainable, without the aid of a charter of incorporation.
Charitable, or public-spirited individuals, desirous of
making permanent appropriations for charitable or other
useful purposes, find it impossible to effect their design
securely, and certainly, without an incorporating act.
They apply to the government, state their beneficent
object, and offer to advance the money necessary for its
accomplishment, provided the government will confer
on the instrument which is to execute their designs the
capacity to execute them. The proposition is considered
and approved. The benefit to the public is considered as
an ample compensation for the faculty it confers, and the
corporation is created. If the advantages to the public
constitute a full compensation for the faculty it gives,
there can be no reason for exacting a further compensation, by claiming a right to exercise over this artificial
being a power which changes its nature, and touches the
fund, for the security and application of which it was
created. There can be no reason for implying in a charter, given for a valuable consideration, a power which is
not only not expressed, but is in direct contradiction to
its express stipulations. . . .

From this review of the charter, it appears that Dartmouth College is an eleemosynary institution, incorporated for the purpose of perpetuating the application of
the bounty of the donors, to the specified objects of that
bounty; that its trustees or governors were originally
named by the founder, and invested with the power of
perpetuating themselves; that they are not public officers,
nor is it a civil institution, participating in the administration of government; but a charity school, or a seminary of education, incorporated for the preservation of
its property, and the perpetual application of that property to the objects of its creation. . . .

Almost all eleemosynary corporations, those which are

created for the promotion of religion, of charity, or of education, are of the same character. The law of this case is the law of all. In every literary or charitable institution, unless the objects of the bounty be themselves incorporated, the whole legal interest is in trustees, and can be asserted only by them. The donors, or claimants of the bounty, if they can appear in court at all, can appear only to complain of the trustees. In all other situations, they are identified with, and personated by, the trustees; and their rights are to be defended and maintained by them. Religion, Charity, and Education, are, in the law of England, legatees or donees, capable of receiving bequests or donations in this form. They appear in court, and claim or defend by the corporation. Are they of so little estimation in the United States that contracts for their benefit must be excluded from the protection of words which, in their natural import, include them? Or do such contracts so necessarily require new-modeling by the authority of the legislature that the ordinary rules of construction must be disregarded in order to leave them exposed to legislative alteration?

All feel that these objects are not deemed unimportant in the United States. The interest which this case has excited proves that they are not. The framers of the constitution did not deem them unworthy of its care and protection. They have, though in a different mode, manifested their respect for science, by reserving to the government of the Union the power "to promote the progress of science and useful arts, by securing for limited times to authors and inventors the exclusive right to their respective writings and discoveries." They have so far withdrawn science, and the useful arts, from the action of the state governments. Why, then, should they be supposed so regardless of contracts made for the advancement of literature as to intend to exclude them from provisions made for the security of ordinary contracts between man and man? No reason for making this supposition is perceived.

If the insignificance of the object does not require that we should exclude contracts respecting it from the pro-

tection of the constitution, neither, as we conceive, is the
policy of leaving them subject to legislative alteration so
apparent as to require a forced construction of that instrument in order to effect it. These eleemosynary institutions do not fill the place, which would otherwise be
occupied by government, but that which would otherwise remain vacant. They are complete acquisitions to
literature. They are donations to education; donations
which any government must be disposed rather to encourage than to discountenance. It requires no very
critical examination of the human mind to enable us to
determine that one great inducement to these gifts is the
conviction felt by the giver, that the disposition he makes
of them is immutable. It is probable that no man ever
was, and that no man ever will be, the founder of a college, believing at the time that an act of incorporation
constitutes no security for the institution; believing that
it is immediately to be deemed a public institution,
whose funds are to be governed and applied, not by the
will of the donor, but by the will of the legislature. All
such gifts are made in the pleasing, perhaps delusive
hope, that the charity will flow forever in the channel
which the givers have marked out for it. If every man
finds in his own bosom strong evidence of the universality of this sentiment, there can be but little reason to
imagine that the framers of our constitution were strang-
ers to it, and that, feeling the necessity and policy of
giving permanence and security to contracts, of withdrawing them from the influence of legislative bodies,
whose fluctuating policy, and repeated interferences, produced the most perplexing and injurious embarrassments,
they still deemed it necessary to leave these contracts subject to those interferences. The motives for such an exception must be very powerful, to justify the construction which makes it. . . .

It has been urged repeatedly, and certainly with a
degree of earnestness which attracted attention, that the
trustees deriving their power from a regal source, must
necessarily partake of the spirit of their origin; and that
their first principles, unimproved by that resplendent

light which has been shed around them, must continue to govern the college, and to guide the students. Before we inquire into the influence which this argument ought to have on the constitutional question, it may not be amiss to examine the fact on which it rests. The first trustees were undoubtedly named in the charter by the crown; but at whose suggestion were they named? By whom were they selected? The charter informs us. Dr. Wheelock had represented "that, for many weighty reasons, it would be expedient that the gentlemen whom he had already nominated in his last will, to be trustees in America, should be of the corporation now proposed." When, afterwards, the trustees are named in the charter, can it be doubted that the persons mentioned by Dr. Wheelock in his will were appointed? Some were probably added by the crown, with the approbation of Dr. Wheelock. Among these is the doctor himself. If any others were appointed at the instance of the crown, they are the governor, three members of the council, and the speaker of the house of representatives of the colony of New Hampshire. The stations filled by these persons ought to rescue them from any other imputation than too great a dependence on the crown. If, in the revolution that followed, they acted under the influence of this sentiment, they must have ceased to be trustees; if they took part with their countrymen, the imputation which suspicion might excite would no longer attach to them. . . .

6. George Ticknor:
Remarks on Changes Lately Proposed or Adopted, in Harvard University *
(1825)

George Ticknor's campaign for reforms to transform Harvard College into a university of European quality was largely unsuccessful. New statutes approved in 1825 were primarily concerned with student discipline, though the elective system was established in Ticknor's own department of modern languages. In commenting on these changes Ticknor predicted that the traditional curriculum would be increasingly inadequate to nineteenth-century needs, pointed to Harvard's unique resources for educational leadership, and criticized the prevailing standards of college teaching.

* George Ticknor, *Remarks on Changes Lately Proposed or Adopted, in Harvard University* ([Boston:] Published by Cummings, Hilliard & Co., 1825), pp. 3–5, 35–36, 44–46. Compare *Statutes and Laws of the University in Cambridge, Massachusetts* (Cambridge, Massachusetts: University Press—Hilliard and Metcalf, 1825). This selection hardly does justice to Ticknor's role as an educational prophet. For further information, see George S. Hilliard, ed., *Life, Letters, and Journals of George Ticknor,* 2 vols. (Boston: J. R. Osgood and Company, 1876); Richard J. Storr, *The Beginnings of Graduate Education in America* (Chicago: University of Chicago Press, 1953), pp. 15–24; Samuel Eliot Morison, "The Great Rebellion in Harvard College, and the Resignation of President Kirkland," in Colonial Society of Massachusetts, *Transactions*, XXVII (1927–30), 54–112; Van Wyck Brooks, *The Flowering of New England, 1815–1865* (New York: E. P. Dutton & Co., 1936), Chapters 2, 4–5; David Bruce Tyack, "Gentleman of Letters: A Study of George Ticknor" (unpublished Ph.D. dissertation, Harvard University, 1958); and

The age in which we live has been appropriately called the age of improvement; and certainly, among the demands made by its peculiar spirit, none has been more constant, more extensive, or more earnest, than the demand, in this country, for an improved state of education. It has been felt among us on every side, and in almost every form; in the humblest primary instruction given by charity; in the large public resorts, where our youth are fitted for the more laborious occupations of life; in our colleges; and in the schools through which the professions are to be entered by those, who hope to attain to much eminence in them. In all, the standard has been greatly raised, and is still rapidly rising, without, perhaps, in any, meeting entirely the wants and hopes of the community. For the generation, on whom now rest the cares of life among us, feel very sensibly, how much more lightly their burthen could be borne, if they had more of that knowledge, which is, indeed, power everywhere, but nowhere so truly and entirely, as in the midst of free institutions; so that there is, at this moment, hardly a father in our country, who does not count among his chief anxieties, and most earnest hopes, the desire to give his children a better education, than he has been able to obtain for himself.

It is natural, and indeed wise, that this stirring spirit should have made very plain and loud demands, on what may be considered the high places of knowledge among us; and it was, perhaps, inevitable, that these demands should first be made in a distinct and definite shape on Harvard College. For Harvard College is one of a very few institutions in our land, that are beginning to be venerable for age and respectable in resources. It is, indeed, the oldest of our greater public schools; it is the most amply endowed; it has, by far, the largest number of teachers; and its collections, libraries, and apparatus,

---

Orrie W. Long, *Thomas Jefferson and George Ticknor: A Chapter in American Scholarship* (Williamstown, Massachusetts: The McClelland Press, 1933), and *Literary Pioneers: Early American Explorers of European Culture* (Cambridge, Massachusetts: Harvard University Press, 1935).

though still very incomplete, are yet, when taken together, more complete than those of any similar establishment in the country. In consequence of this, and in
consequence of a general persuasion, that this ancient
establishment has not fulfilled the expectations and
claims, which its increased means have excited, important
discussions have been carried on for some years back by
those to whose management its affairs are entrusted, concerning its organisation, discipline, and instruction, in
the hope of fitting it better to the increased and increasing demands of the community.

The discussions brought out by this state of feeling and
opinion, have laid before the public the means and management of this college more fully than, from official
sources, the means and management of any college in the
country had been known before. An indistinct persuasion
had, indeed, long prevailed, that it did not keep pace
with the spirit of the times, and that a considerable portion of its means was not brought into efficient operation;
but the exaggerated fears and statements, to which this
uncertainty gave rise, are now removed, and from the
authentic sources, which are become accessible to all,
the following may be easily distinguished as among the
principal grounds for the anxiety, which prevailed in regard to its existing condition; and may serve, at the same
time, as a warning to most of the other colleges in our
country, which, in proportion to their respective ages
and means, are advancing with the same system and the
same usages to similar results.

In the *first* place, the time really appropriated to study,
and provided with means of instruction, is found to have
been too small, owing to the great amount of vacations
and holidays. . . .

In the *next* place, even during the time appropriated
to study, and regularly filled with recitations, the modes
of instruction are found to have been imperfect, compared with the means, from which they were furnished.
The whole system of instruction has, heretofore, rested
on the alphabetical arrangement of the four classes; as
if a young man's talent and character depended on the

letter with which his name happens to begin. This was a radical and capital defect. The attempt to force together sixty or eighty young men, many of whom have nothing, or almost nothing, in common; who are of very unequal ages, talents, attainments, habits, and characters; and to compel them to advance *pari passu* during four of the most active and valuable years of life, giving to the most industrious and intelligent no more and no other lessons, than to the most dull and idle, is a thing that is unknown to the practical arrangements for education in other countries; that is not attempted in ours either before or after the period of college life; and that has been practised at college only from adherence to an ancient arrangement, long after the motives for that arrangement had ceased to exist. . . .

[There] is now before the public . . . a code of Laws, called "Statutes and Laws of the University in Cambridge, Massachusetts," embraced in about forty pages and an hundred and fifty-three separate regulations, which, on account of the important changes it proposes, and the influence they may be likely to exercise, it is proposed now partly to examine.

In the *first* place, then, Harvard College is now, by the eleventh section of its present laws, thrown open to all who wish to obtain any of the instruction it offers, whether they intend to seek an academic degree or not. This seems to be an important and beneficial regulation. An institution, while it is poor and has few teachers, may be compelled, from the necessity of the case, or from the great inconveniences attending a different mode, to confine its instructions to a strictly marked course, the end of which is limited by a merely formal and unmeaning certificate. But a college of large means and numerous instructers, has no apology for thus embarrassing and restricting its usefulness. It should open its doors to all; for, if its resources be properly and efficiently applied, it has means of instruction for all.

Harvard College has abundant resources to render unnecessary the establishment of many public and private institutions, like the agricultural schools, the law schools, and the other establishments for special purposes, which like the admirable and flourishing institution at Gardiner, in Maine, are already beginning or begun among us also. These are not to be complained of; on the contrary, they are subjects of congratulation; but it is obvious, that, if Harvard College would put forth its unused means, it could accomplish at once and better, much of what they can bring to pass, only slowly and imperfectly with great labour. For such instructions must be had among us. The great increase of manufacturing establishments, which all require men of peculiar skill and knowledge to manage them; the improvement in all the arts, which supposes a corresponding improvement in the education of those who are devoted to them; and the practical intelligence and general character of the whole country, which demands, in its best sense, a liberal education for many persons in all classes of the community;—all these have long since made requisitions on our best places for public education, which have not yet been fully answered at any of them, but which the general uneasiness will not suffer to remain unanswered much longer. And it is at once the duty and the interest of a large institution like Cambridge, to meet this demand; to make its resources minister freely to a much wider usefulness than is now thought of; and to extend effectual instruction to portions of society that now never resort there; for, while it is conferring all these benefits, it will, of course, be increased in the number of its students, and be strengthened in the interests and good will of the community, by having its basis so much more broadly and firmly laid in the very constitution of our society. . . .

But there is one point that, I believe, must be made a sort of cynosure, when beneficial changes are undertaken, both at Harvard and at our other colleges; and that is, the principle of thorough TEACHING. On this point, it is desirable to be perfectly plain, and to be very plainly understood. It is a small matter to diminish the unreasonable amount of holidays, or to give the students more and longer lessons, under a division according to proficiency, or to do almost any thing else, if the principle of *teaching* is still to be overlooked. For the most that an instructer now undertakes in our colleges, is, to ascertain from day to day, whether the young men who are assembled in his presence, have probably studied the lesson prescribed to them. There his duty stops. If the lesson have been learnt, it is well; if it have not, nothing remains but punishment, after a sufficient number of such offences shall have been accumulated to demand it; and then it comes halting after the delinquent, he hardly knows why. The idea of a thorough commentary on the lesson; the idea of making the explanations and illustrations of the teacher, of as much consequence as the recitation of the book, or even of more, is substantially unknown in this country, except at a few preparatory schools. The consequence is, that, though many of our colleges may have a valuable apparatus for instruction; though they may be very good, quiet and secluded places for study; and though many of the young men who resort thither, may really learn not a little of what is exacted or expected from them; yet, after all, not one of our colleges is a place for thorough *teaching;* and not one of the better class of them does half of what it might do, by bringing the minds of its instructers to act directly and vigorously on the minds of its pupils, and thus to encourage, enable and compel them to learn what they ought to learn, and what they easily might learn.

Consider only, that as many years are given to the great work of education here as are given in Europe; and that it costs more money with us to be very imperfectly educated than it does to enjoy the great advantages of some of the best institutions and universities on the continent. And yet, who, in this country, by means here offered him, has been enabled to make himself a good Greek scholar? Who has been taught thoroughly to read, write, and speak Latin? Nay, who has been taught anything at our colleges with the thoroughness that will enable him to go safely and directly onward to distinction in the department he has thus entered without returning to lay anew the foundations for his success? It is a shame to be obliged to ask such questions; and yet

there is but one answer to them, and those, who have
visited and examined the great schools of Europe have
bitterly felt there, what this answer is, and why it must
be given.

In some of our colleges, there may be a reason for this
state of things. Their means are small; their apparatus incomplete; their instructers few. They do what they can;
but they cannot do much more than spread before their
students a small part of the means for acquiring knowledge, examine them sufficiently to ascertain their general
diligence, and encourage them to exertion by such rewards and punishments as they can command. And in
doing this, they may do the community great service and
honourably fulfil their own duties. But at Cambridge
and at our larger colleges much more than this can be
done and ought to be done. The young men may be
taught as well as examined. The large apparatus of Libraries, instruments and collections, and the greater
number of Professors and Tutors may be turned to much
better account and made to produce much wider and
more valuable results. The increasing demands of the
community may be here met; and our high places for
education may easily accommodate themselves more
wisely to the spirit and wants of the times in which we
live. And this if done at all, must be done speedily; for
new institutions are springing up, which, in the flexibil-
ity of their youth, will easily take the forms that are required of them, while the older establishments, if they
suffer themselves to grow harder and harder in their ancient habits and systems, will find, when the period for
more important alterations is come and free Universities
are demanded and called forth, that, instead of being
able to place themselves at the head of the coming
changes and directing their course, they will only be the
first victims of the spirit of improvement.

7.   The Yale Report*
(1828)

Responding to the challenge presented by the University of Virginia and by appeals for curricular expansion, electives, and the development of comprehensive universities from Harvard, Amherst, Union, and Vermont during the 1820's, the Yale faculty issued an uncompromising defense of the prescribed curriculum and the residential college, which remained the chief reliance of educational conservatives until after the Civil War. This section of the report was the work of President Jeremiah Day (1773–1867).

The guardians of the college appear to have ever acted upon the principle, that it ought not to be stationary, but continually advancing. Some alteration has accordingly been proposed, almost every year, from its first establishment. It is with no small surprise, therefore, we occasionally hear the suggestion, that our system is unalterable; that colleges were originally planned, in the days of monkish ignorance; and that, "by being immovably moored to the same station, they serve only to measure

* "Original Papers in Relation to a Course of Liberal Education," *The American Journal of Science and the Arts,* XV, January 1829, 299–303, 308–313, 315, 317–320. On the significance of the Report, see George P. Schmidt, "Intellectual Crosscurrents in American Colleges, 1825–1855," *The American Historical Review,* XLII, October 1936, 46–67, and R. Freeman Butts, *The College Charts Its Course: Historical Conceptions and Current Proposals* (New York: McGraw-Hill Book Company, Inc., 1939), Chapter 7. For a later restatement of Yale's educational traditionalism, see Noah Porter, *The American Colleges and the American Public,* new ed. (New York: C. Scribner's Sons, 1878).

the rapid current of improvement which is passing by them."

How opposite to all this, is the real state of facts, in this and the other seminaries in the United States. Nothing is more common, than to hear those who revisit the college, after a few years absence, express their surprise at the changes which have been made since they were graduated. Not only the course of studies, and the modes of instruction, have been greatly varied; but whole sciences have, for the first time, been introduced; chemistry, mineralogy, geology, political economy, &c. By raising the qualifications for admission, the standard of attainment has been elevated. Alterations so extensive and frequent, satisfactorily prove, that if those who are intrusted with the superintendence of the institution, still firmly adhere to some of its original features, it is from a higher principle, than a blind opposition to salutary reform. Improvements, we trust, will continue to be made, as rapidly as they can be, without hazarding the loss of what has been already attained.

But perhaps the time has come, when we ought to pause, and inquire, whether it will be sufficient to make *gradual* changes, as heretofore; and whether the whole system is not rather to be broken up, and a better one substituted in its stead. From different quarters, we have heard the suggestion, that our colleges must be *new-modelled;* that they are not adapted to the spirit and wants of the age; that they will soon be deserted, unless they are better accommodated to the business character of the nation. As this point may have an important bearing upon the question immediately before the committee, we would ask their indulgence, while we attempt to explain, at some length, the nature and object of the present plan of education at the college.

We shall in vain attempt to decide on the expediency of retaining or altering our present course of instruction, unless we have a distinct apprehension of the *object* of a collegiate education. A plan of study may be well adapted to a particular purpose, though it may be very unsuitable for a different one. Universities, colleges, academical, and professional seminaries, ought not to be all constituted upon the same model; but should be so varied as to attain the ends which they have severally in view.

What then is the appropriate object of a college? It is not necessary here to determine what it is which, in every case, entitles an institution to the *name* of a college. But if we have not greatly misapprehended the design of the patrons and guardians of this college, its object is to LAY THE FOUNDATION OF a SUPERIOR EDUCATION: and this is to be done, at a period of life when a substitute must be provided for *parental superintendence*. The ground work of a thorough education, must be broad, and deep, and solid. For a partial or superficial education, the support may be of looser materials, and more hastily laid.

The two great points to be gained in intellectual culture, are the *discipline* and the *furniture* of the mind; expanding its powers, and storing it with knowledge. The former of these is, perhaps, the more important of the two. A commanding object, therefore, in a collegiate course, should be, to call into daily and vigorous exercise the faculties of the student. Those branches of study should be prescribed, and those modes of instruction adopted, which are best calculated to teach the art of fixing the attention, directing the train of thought, analyzing a subject proposed for investigation; following, with accurate discrimination, the course of argument; balancing nicely the evidence presented to the judgment; awakening, elevating, and controlling the imagination; arranging, with skill, the treasures which memory gathers; rousing and guiding the powers of genius. All this is not to be effected by a light and hasty course of study; by reading a few books, hearing a few lectures, and spending some months at a literary institution. The habits of thinking are to be formed, by long continued and close application. The mines of science must be penetrated far below the surface, before they will disclose their treasures. If a dexterous performance of the manual operations, in many of the mechanical arts, requires an apprenticeship, with diligent attention for years; much more does the training of the powers of the mind demand vigorous, and steady, and systematic effort.

In laying the foundation of a thorough education, it is necessary that *all* the important mental faculties be brought into exercise. It is not sufficient that one or two be cultivated, while others are neglected. A costly edifice ought not to be left to rest upon a single pillar. When certain mental endowments receive a much higher culture than others, there is a distortion in the intellectual character. The mind never attains its full perfection, unless its various powers are so trained as to give them the fair proportions which nature designed. If the student exercises his reasoning powers only, he will be deficient in imagination and taste, in fervid and impressive eloquence. If he confines his attention to demonstrative evidence, he will be unfitted to decide correctly, in cases of probability. If he relies principally on his memory, his powers of invention will be impaired by disuse. In the course of instruction in this college, it has been an object to maintain such a proportion between the different branches of literature and science, as to form in the student a proper *balance* of character. From the pure mathematics, he learns the art of demonstrative reasoning. In attending to the physical sciences, he becomes familiar with facts, with the process of induction, and the varieties of probable evidence. In ancient literature, he finds some of the most finished models of taste. By English reading, he learns the powers of the language in which he is to speak and write. By logic and mental philosophy, he is taught the art of thinking; by rhetoric and oratory, the art of speaking. By frequent exercise on written composition, he acquires copiousness and accuracy of expression. By extemporaneous discussion, he becomes prompt, and fluent, and animated. It is a point of high importance, that eloquence and solid learning should go together; that he who has accumulated the richest treasures of thought, should possess the highest powers of oratory. To what purpose has a man become deeply learned, if he has no faculty of communicating his knowledge? And of what use is a display of rhetorical elegance, from one who knows little or nothing which is worth communicating? Est enim scientia comprehendenda rerum plurimarum, sine qua verborum volubilitas inanis atque irridenda est. Cic. Our course, therefore, aims at a union of science with literature; of solid attainment with skill in the art of persuasion.

No one feature in a system of intellectual education, is of greater moment than such an arrangement of duties and motives, as will most effectually throw the student upon the *resources of his own mind*. Without this, the whole apparatus of libraries, and instruments, and specimens, and lectures, and teachers, will be insufficient to secure distinguished excellence. The scholar must form himself, by his own exertions. The advantages furnished by a residence at a college, can do little more than stimulate and aid his personal efforts. The *inventive* powers are especially to be called into vigorous exercise. However abundant may be the acquisitions of the student, if he has no talent at forming new combinations of thought, he will be dull and inefficient. The sublimest efforts of genius consist in the creations of the imagination, the discoveries of the intellect, the conquests by which the dominions of science are extended. But the culture of the inventive faculties is not the *only* object of a liberal education. The most gifted understanding cannot greatly enlarge the amount of science to which the wisdom of ages has contributed. If it were possible for a youth to have his faculties in the highest state of cultivation, without any of the knowledge which is derived from others, he would be but poorly fitted for the business of life. To the discipline of the mind, therefore, is to be added instruction. The analytic method must be combined with the synthetic. Analysis is most efficacious in directing the powers of invention; but is far too slow in its progress to teach, within a moderate space of time, the circle of the sciences.

In our arrangements for the communication of knowledge, as well as in intellectual discipline, such branches are to be taught as will produce a proper symmetry and balance of character. We doubt whether the powers of the mind can be developed, in their fairest proportions, by studying languages alone, or mathematics alone, or natural or political science alone. As the bodily frame is brought to its highest perfection, not by one simple and uniform motion, but by a variety of exercises; so the mental faculties are expanded, and invigorated, and adapted to each other, by familiarity with different departments of science.

A most important feature in the colleges of this country is, that the students are generally of an age which requires, that a substitute be provided for *parental superintendence*. When removed from under the roof of their parents, and exposed to the untried scenes of temptation, it is necessary that some faithful and affectionate guardian take them by the hand, and guide their steps. This consideration determines the *kind* of government which ought to be maintained in our colleges. As it is a substitute for the regulations of a family, it should approach as near to the character of parental control as the circumstances of the case will admit. It should be founded on mutual affection and confidence. It should aim to effect its purpose, principally by kind and persuasive influence; not wholly or chiefly by restraint and terror. Still, punishment may sometimes be necessary. There may be perverse members of a college, as well as of a family. There may be those whom nothing but the arm of law can reach.

The parental character of college government, requires that the students should be so collected together, as to constitute one family; that the intercourse between them and their instructers may be frequent and familiar. This renders it necessary that suitable *buildings* be provided, for the residence of the students:—we speak now of colleges in the country, the members of which are mostly gathered from a distance. In a large city, where the students reside with their parents, public rooms only are needed. This may be the case also, in professional institutions, in which the students are more advanced in age, and, therefore, do not require a minute superintendence on the part of their instructers. . . .

The collegiate course of study, of which we have now given a summary view, we hope may be carefully distinguished from several *other* objects and plans, with which it has been too often confounded. It is far from embracing *every thing* which the student will ever have occasion to learn. The object is not to *finish* his education; but to lay the foundation, and to advance as far in rearing the superstructure, as the short period of his residence here will admit. If he acquires here a thorough knowledge of the principles of science, he may then, in a great measure, educate himself. He has, at least, been taught *how* to learn. With the aid of books, and means of observation, he may be constantly advancing in knowledge. Wherever he goes, into whatever company he falls, he has those general views, on every topic of interest, which will enable him to understand, to digest, and to form a correct opinion, on the statements and discussions which he hears. There are many things important to be known, which are not taught in colleges, because they may be learned any where. The knowledge, though indispensable, comes to us as freely, in the way of our business, as our necessary supplies of light, and air, and water.

The course of instruction which is given to the undergraduates in the college, is not designed to include *professional* studies. Our object is not to teach that which is peculiar to any one of the professions; but to lay the foundation which is common to them all. There are separate schools for medicine, law, and theology, connected with the college, as well as in various parts of the country; which are open for the reception of all who are prepared to enter upon the appropriate studies of their several professions. With these, the academical course is not intended to interfere.

But why, it may be asked, should a student waste his time upon studies which have no immediate connection with his future profession? Will chemistry enable him to plead at the bar, or conic sections qualify him for preaching, or astronomy aid him in the practice of physic? Why should not his attention be confined to the subject which is to occupy the labors of his life? In answer to this, it may be observed, that there is no science which does not contribute its aid to professional skill. "Every thing throws light upon every thing." The great object of a collegiate education, preparatory to the study of a profession, is to give that expansion and balance of the mental powers, those liberal and comprehensive views, and those fine proportions of character, which are not to be found in him whose ideas are always confined to one particular channel. When a man has entered upon the practice of his profession, the energies of his mind must be given, principally, to its appropriate duties. But if his thoughts never range on other subjects, if he never looks abroad on the ample domains of literature and science, there will be a narrowness in his habits of thinking, a peculiarity of character, which will be sure to mark him as a man of limited views and attainments. Should he be distinguished in his profession, his ignorance on other subjects, and the defects of his education, will be the more exposed to public observation. On the other hand, he who is not only eminent in professional life, but has also a mind richly stored with general knowledge, has an elevation and dignity of character, which gives him a commanding influence in society, and a widely extended sphere of usefulness. His situation enables him to diffuse the light of science among all classes of the community. Is a man to have no other object, than to obtain a *living* by professional pursuits? Has he not duties to perform to his family, to his fellow citizens, to his country; duties which require various and extensive intellectual furniture?

Professional studies are designedly excluded from the course of instruction at college, to leave room for those literary and scientific acquisitions which, if not commenced there, will, in most cases, never be made. They will not grow up spontaneously, amid the bustle of business. We are not here speaking of those giant minds which, by their native energy, break through the obstructions of a defective education, and cut their own path to distinction. These are honorable exceptions to the general law; not examples for common imitation. Franklins and Marshalls are not found in sufficient numbers to fill a college. And even Franklin would not have been what he was, if there had been no colleges in the country. When an elevated standard of education is maintained, by the higher literary institutions, men of superior powers, who have not had access to these, are stimulated to aim at a similar elevation, by their own efforts, and by aid of the light which is thus shining around them.

As our course of instruction is not intended to complete an education, in theological, medical, or legal science; neither does it include all the minute details of *mercantile, mechanical,* or *agricultural* concerns. These can never be effectually learned except in the very circumstances in which they are to be practised. The young merchant must be trained in the counting room, the mechanic, in the workshop, the farmer, in the field. But we have, on our premises, no experimental farm or retail shop; no cotton or iron manufactory; no hatter's, or silver-smith's, or coach-maker's establishment. For what purpose, then, it will be asked, are young men who are destined to these occupations, ever sent to a college? They should not be sent, as we think, with an expectation of *finishing* their education at the college; but with a view of laying a thorough foundation in the principles of science, preparatory to the study of the practical arts. As every thing cannot be learned in four years, either theory or practice must be, in a measure at least, postponed to a future opportunity. But if the scientific theory of the arts is *ever* to be acquired, it is unquestionably first in order of time. The corner stone must be laid, before the superstructure is erected. If suitable arrangements were made, the details of mercantile, mechanical, and agricultural education, might be taught at the college, to *resident graduates.* Practical skill would then be grounded upon scientific information.

The question may be asked, What is a young man fitted for, when he takes his degree? Does he come forth from the college qualified for business? We answer, no,— if he stops here. His education is begun, but not completed. Is the college to be reproached for not accom-

plishing that which it has never undertaken to perform?
Do we complain of the mason, who has laid the foundation of a house, that he has done nothing to purpose;
that he has not finished the building; that the product
of his labor is not habitable; and that, therefore, there is
nothing practical in what he has done? Do we say of the
planter, who has raised a crop of cotton, that he has
done nothing practical, because he has not given to his
product the form of wearing apparel?

In education, as well as in morals, we often hear the
suggestion, that principles are of no consequence, provided the practice is right. Why waste on theories, the
time which is wanted for acquiring practical arts? We
are aware, that some operations may be performed, by
those who have little or no knowledge of the principles
on which they depend. The mariner may set his sails to
the wind, without understanding the laws of the decomposition of forces; the carpenter may square his framework, without a knowledge of Euclid's Elements; the
dyer may set his colors, without being indoctrinated in
the principles of chemistry. But the labors of such an
one, are confined to the narrow path marked out to him
by others. He needs the constant superintendence of men
of more enlarged and scientific information. If he ven-
tures beyond his prescribed rule, he works at random,
with no established principles to guide him. By long continued practice, he may have attained a good degree of
manual dexterity. But the arranging of plans of business,
the new combinations of mechanical processes, the discoveries and improvements in the arts, must generally
come from minds more highly and systematically cultivated. There is a fertility in scientific principles, of which
the mere artist has no apprehension. A single general law
may include a thousand or ten thousand particular cases;
each one of which is as difficult to be learned or remem-
bered, as the law which explains them all. Men of mere
practical detail are wanted, in considerable numbers, to
fill the subordinate places in mechanical establishments;
but the higher stations require enlightened and comprehensive views.

We are far from believing that theory *alone,* should be taught in a college. It cannot be effectually taught, except in connection with practical illustrations. These are necessary in exciting an interest in theoretical instructions; and especially important in showing the application of principles. It is our aim therefore, while engaged in scientific investigations, to blend with them, as far as possible, practical illustrations and experiments. Of what use are all the sublime discoveries which have immortalized the names of Newton, Archimedes, and others; if the principles which they have unfolded, are never to be taught to those who can reduce them to practice? Why do we bestow such exalted encomiums on inventive genius, if the results of original investigations, are to be confined to a few scientific men, and not diffused among those who are engaged in the active duties of life? To bring down the principles of science to their practical application by the laboring classes, is the office of men of superior education. It is the separation of theory and practice, which has brought reproach upon both. Their union alone can elevate them to their true dignity and value. The man of science is often disposed to assume an air of superiority, when he looks upon the narrow and partial views of the mere artisan. The latter in return laughs at the practical blunders of the former. The defects in the education of both classes would be remedied, by giving them a knowledge of scientific principles, preparatory to practice.

We are aware that a thorough education is not within the reach of all. Many, for want of time and pecuniary resources, must be content with a partial course. A defective education is better than none. If a youth can afford to devote only two or three years, to a scientific and professional education, it will be proper for him to make a selection of a few of the most important branches, and give his attention exclusively to these. But this is an imperfection, arising from the necessity of the case. A partial course of study, must inevitably give a partial education.

This, we are well convinced, is far preferable to a

superficial education. Of all the plans of instruction which have been offered to the public, that is the most preposterous, which proposes to teach almost every thing in a short time. In this way, nothing is effectually taught. The pupil is hurried over the surface so rapidly, that scarce a trace of his steps remains, when he has finished his course. What he has learned, or thinks he has learned, is just sufficient to inflate his vanity, to expose him to public observation, and to draw on him the ridicule of men of sound judgment and science. A partial education is often expedient; a superficial one, never. Whatever a young man undertakes to learn, however little it may be, he ought to learn it so effectually, that it may be of some practical use to him. If there is any way in which every thing worth knowing may be taught in four years, we are free to acknowledge, that we are not in possession of the secret.

But why, it is asked, should *all* the students in a college be required to tread in the *same steps?* Why should not each one be allowed to select those branches of study which are most to his taste, which are best adapted to his peculiar talents, and which are most nearly connected with his intended profession? To this we answer, that our prescribed course contains those subjects only which ought to be understood, as we think, by every one who aims at a thorough education. They are not the peculiarities of any profession or art. These are to be learned in the professional and practical schools. But the principles of science, are the common foundation of all high intellectual attainments. As in our primary schools, reading, writing, and arithmetic are taught to all, however different their prospects; so in a college, all should be instructed in those branches of knowledge, of which no one destined to the higher walks of life ought to be ignorant. What subject which is now studied here, could be set aside, without evidently marring the system. Not to speak particularly, in this place, of the ancient languages; who that aims at a well proportioned and superior education will remain ignorant of the elements of the various branches of the mathematics, or of history

and antiquities, or of rhetoric and oratory, or natural
philosophy, or astronomy, or chemistry, or mineralogy,
or geology, or political economy, or mental and moral
philosophy?

It is sometimes thought that a student ought not to be
urged to the study of that for which he has *no taste or
capacity*. But how is he to know, whether he has a taste
or capacity for a science, before he has even entered upon
its elementary truths? If he is really destitute of talent
sufficient for these common departments of education, he
is destined for some narrow sphere of action. But we are
well persuaded, that our students are not so deficient in
intellectual powers, as they sometimes profess to be;
though they are easily made to believe, that they have
no capacity for the study of that which they are told is
almost wholly useless. . . .

The Universities on the continent of Europe, especially
in Germany, have of late gained the notice and respect
of men of information in this country. They are upon a
broad and liberal scale, affording very great facilities for
a finished education. But we doubt whether they are
models to be copied in every feature, by our American
colleges. We hope at least, that this college may be
spared the mortification of a ludicrous attempt to imitate
them, while it is unprovided with the resources necessary
to execute the purpose. The only institution in this country, which, so far as we know, has started upon the plan
of the European universities,* required an expenditure,
before commencing operations, of more than three hundred thousand dollars; a sum far greater than Yale College has received in a century and a quarter, from the
bounty of individuals and the state together. The students come to the universities in Germany at a more advanced age, and with much higher preparatory attainments, than to the colleges in this country. The period of
education which is there divided into *two* portions only,
one of which is spent at the gymnasium and the other at
the university, is here divided into *three,* that of the
grammar school, the college, and the professional school.

* The University of Virginia.—T.R.C.

The pupils, when they enter the university, are advanced nearly or quite as far, in literature if not in science, as our students are when graduated. The institution in Germany which corresponds most nearly to our colleges, in point of attainments, and the age of the students, is the gymnasium. The universities are mostly occupied with *professional* studies. . . .

One of the pleas frequently urged in favor of a partial education, is the alleged *want of time* for a more enlarged course. We are well aware, as we have already observed, that a thorough education cannot be begun and finished in four years. But if three years immediately preceding the age of twenty-one be allowed for the study of a profession, there is abundant time previous to this for the attainment of all which is now required for admission into the college, in addition to the course prescribed for the undergraduates. Though the limit of age for admission is fixed by our laws at fourteen, yet how often have we been pressed to dispense with the rule, in behalf of some youth who has completed his preparation at an earlier period; and who, if compelled to wait till he has attained the requisite age, "is in danger of being ruined for want of employment?" May we not expect, that this plea will be urged with still greater earnestness, when the present improved methods of instruction in the elementary and preparatory schools, are more and more accelerating the early progress of the pupil?

But suppose it should happen that the student, in consequence of commencing his studies at a later period, should be delayed a little longer, before entering upon the duties of his profession; is this a sacrifice worthy to be compared with the immense difference between the value of a limited and a thorough education? Is a young man's pushing forward into business, so indispensable to his future welfare, that rather than suspend it for a single year, he must forego all the advantage of superior intellectual discipline and attainments?

We well know that the whole population of the country can never enjoy the benefit of a thorough course of education. A large portion must be content with the very limited instruction in our primary schools. Others may be able to add to this the privilege of a few months at an academy. Others still, with higher aims and more ample means, may afford to spend two or three years, in attending upon a partial course of study, in some institution which furnishes instruction in any branch or branches selected by the pupil or his parents.

The question is then presented, whether the college shall have all the variety of classes and departments which are found in academies; or whether it shall confine itself to the single object of a well proportioned and thorough course of study. It is said that the public now demand, that the doors should be thrown open to all; that education ought to be so modified, and varied, as to adapt it to the exigencies of the country, and the prospects of different individuals; that the instruction given to those who are destined to be merchants, or manufacturers, or agriculturalists, should have a special reference to their respective professional pursuits.

The public are undoubtedly right, in demanding that there should be appropriate courses of education, accessible to all classes of youth. And we rejoice at the prospect of ample provision for this purpose, in the improvement of our academies, and the establishment of commercial high-schools, gymnasia, lycea, agricultural seminaries, &c. But do the public insist, that every college shall become a high-school, gymnasium, lyceum, and academy? Why should we interfere with these valuable institutions? Why wish to take their business out of their hands? The college has its appropriate object, and they have theirs. What advantage would be gained by attempting to blend them all in one? When in almost all our schools, and academies, and professional seminaries, the standard of education has been enlarged and elevated, is this a time for the college to *lower* its standard? Shall we fall back, and abandon the ground which, for thirty years past, we have been striving so hard to gain? Are those who are seeking only a partial education to be admitted into the college, merely for the purpose of associating its *name* with theirs? of carrying away with them a collegiate *diploma,* without incurring the fearful hazard of being over-educated? Why is a degree from a college more highly prized, than a certificate from an academy, if the former is not a voucher of a superior education? When the course of instruction in the one, is reduced to the level of that in the other; to be graduated at either, will be equally honorable. What is the characteristic difference between a college and an academy? Not that the former teaches more branches than the latter. There are many academies in the country, whose scheme of studies, at least upon paper, is more various that that of the colleges. But while an academy teaches a little of every thing, the college, by directing its efforts to one uniform course, aims at doing its work with greater precision, and economy of time; just as the merchant who deals in a single class of commodities, or a manufacturer who produces but one kind of fabrics, executes his business more perfectly, than he whose attention and skill are divided among a multitude of objects.

If our treasury were overflowing, if we had a *surplus fund,* requiring us to look out for some new object on which to expend it, there might perhaps be no harm in establishing a department for a brief and rapid course of study, so far connected with the college, as to be under the superintendence of the same board of trust. But it ought to be as distinct from the four classes of undergraduates, as is the medical or law school. All the means which are now applied to the proper collegiate department, are barely sufficient, or rather are insufficient, for the object in view. No portion of our resources, or strength, or labor, can be diverted to other purposes, without impairing the education which we are attempting to give. A London university, commencing with a capital of several hundred thousand dollars, and aiming to provide a system of instruction for the youth in a city whose population is more than a million, may well establish its higher and inferior courses, its scientific and practical departments, its professional, mercantile, and mechanical institutions. But shall a college, with an income of two or three thousand a year from funds, affect to be

at once a London university? Should we *ever* become
such an institution, our present undergraduate course,
ought still to constitute one distinct branch of the com-
plicated system of arrangements.

But might we not, by making the college more accessible to different descriptions of persons, enlarge our
numbers, and in that way, increase our income? This
might be the operation of the measure, for a very short
time, while a degree from the college should retain its
present value in public estimation; a value depending
entirely upon the character of the education which we
give. But the moment it is understood that the institution has descended to an inferior standard of attainment,
its reputation will sink to a corresponding level. After
we shall have become a college in *name only,* and in
reality nothing more than an academy; or half college,
and half academy; what will induce parents in various
and distant parts of the country, to send us their sons,
when they have academies enough in their own neighborhood? There is no magical influence in an act of incorporation, to give celebrity to a literary institution,
which does not command respect for itself, by the elevated rank of its education. When the college has lost its
hold on the public confidence, by depressing its standard
of merit, by substituting a partial, for a thorough education, we may expect that it will be deserted by that class
of persons who have hitherto been drawn here by high
expectations and purposes. Even if we should *not* immediately suffer in point of *numbers,* yet we shall ex-
change the best portion of our students, for others of inferior aims and attainments.

As long as we can maintain an elevated character, we
need be under no apprehension with respect to numbers.
Without character, it will be in vain to think of retaining
them. It is a hazardous experiment, to act upon the plan
of gaining numbers first, and character afterwards. . . .

8. Denominationalism:
William S. Tyler,
*Prayer for Colleges** (1855)

Sectarian rivalry provided the major impetus for the founding of new American colleges after 1815. The Society for the Promotion of Collegiate and Theological Education at the West, established in 1843, coordinated appeals for eastern funds and directed support to the strongest of the new western institutions, principally Congregational or Presbyterian offshoots of Yale and Princeton in areas of the upper Mississippi Valley settled by New Englanders. The following essay contains the principal arguments for denominational higher education. It was written by William Seymour Tyler (1810–1897), Professor of Greek at Amherst College.

* W. S. Tyler, *Prayer for Colleges. A Premium Essay, Written for "The Society for the Promotion of Collegiate and Theological Education at the West"* (New York: Published by M. W. Dodd, for the Society, 1855), pp. 102–112, 116–120. On Tyler, see *Dictionary of American Biography*, Vol. XIX, pp. 99–100. For additional examples of the promotional literature of sectarian colleges, see Lyman Beecher, *A Plea for the West* (Cincinnati: Truman and Smith, 1835), and *A Plea for Colleges*, 2nd ed. (Cincinnati: Published by Truman and Smith, and New York: By Leavitt, Lord and Co., 1836); and Noah Porter, *The Educational Systems of the Puritans and Jesuits Compared, A Premium Essay Written for "The Society for the Promotion of Collegiate and Theological Education at the West"* (New York: M. W. Dodd, 1851). For discussion of denominationalism and higher education, see Donald G. Tewksbury, *The Founding of American Colleges and Universities Before the Civil War, With Particular Reference to the Religious Influences Bearing on the College Movement* (New York: Bureau of Publications, Teachers College, Columbia University, 1932); and Richard Hofstadter and Walter P. Metzger, *The Development of Academic Freedom in the United States* (New York: Columbia University Press, 1955), Chapter 5.

Schools and colleges, wherever they exist, almost without exception, owe their origin to the church. Christianity is, in its very nature, friendly to learning. It is a religion not of forms and of ceremonies, but of the mind and heart. It saves men, not by outward means and appliances, but by the inward workings of the truth and the Spirit of God in their souls. Knowledge is, therefore, essential to holiness and salvation. Its ministry is a teaching and preaching ministry, not a mere officiating and manipulating priesthood. Its sacred books contain not only the most stirring truths, and the most commanding motives, but the choicest specimens of history, poetry and philosophy, the world has ever seen; and those, too, originally communicated in a foreign language, and for this reason, as well as many others, requiring prolonged study and extensive knowledge, in order to their full understanding and appreciation. Christianity produces an inquiring, observing, thinking and intelligent laity. It demands a reading, studying, reflecting and learned ministry.

The first ministers of the gospel were taught immediately by Christ, and were, moreover, constantly under the especial divine teaching of the Holy Spirit. They, therefore, stood in little need of human learning. Yet one of the apostles, and one who exceeded all the others in his labors and usefulness, was taught in the best Jewish and Gentile schools of Jerusalem and Tarsus. And no sooner were the miraculous gifts, which signalized the first establishment of Christianity, withdrawn, than the churches began to found colleges and theological schools at Jerusalem and Alexandria, and the other principal cities, for the especial purpose of raising up a pious and learned ministry, who should be able not only to preach the truth to its friends, but also to defend it from the assaults of its adversaries. And though, during the middle ages, learning every where suffered a disastrous eclipse, yet what light there was, shone from the schools in the monasteries, which were established by such enlightened and pious princes as Charlemagne and Alfred, chiefly for the elevation of the clergy, and which gradually grew up into universities. As this eclipse passed off slowly, and universities began to appear in Italy, in France, in England, they were established and fostered by the church, and chiefly for the better education of the clergy. Oxford and Cambridge were founded, and in the course of time enriched with princely endowments for this express purpose. Zeal for religion conspired with love of learning, and college after college was added to those ancient and venerable universities, chiefly for the charitable education of intelligent young men for the service of the church.

The necessity for a well-educated ministry of the gospel has never been so generally and powerfully felt any where else as in our own country; and this feeling has been the leading motive in the establishment of by far the larger part of American colleges. "Dreading to leave an illiterate ministry to the churches, when our ministers shall lie in the dust"—such is the language in which the founders of Harvard College describe their own motives in that far-seeing and self-denying enterprise, which they undertook just as soon as they had provided comfortable houses for themselves, and selected convenient places for the worship of God. And sixty years later, Cotton Mather says: "Our fathers saw that without a college to train an able and learned ministry, the church in New England must have been less than a business of an age,—must soon have come to nothing." "Pro Christo et Ecclesia" —*for Christ and the Church*—is to this day the motto of Harvard College, though sadly fallen, alas! from the truth as it is in Jesus.

Yale College, as we have already mentioned, was founded by ministers. It was also founded chiefly for the education of ministers for the colony of Connecticut. It originated, as they tell us, in their sincere regard and zeal for upholding the Protestant religion by a succession of learned and orthodox men.

"Princeton College was founded by the Synod of New York for the purpose of supplying the church with learned and able preachers of the Word." And its paramount religious design and spirit are well expressed in the language of President Witherspoon: "Cursed be all that learning that is contrary to the cross of Christ; cursed be all that learning that is not coincident with the cross of Christ; cursed be all that learning that is not subservient to the cross of Christ."

"Dartmouth College was originated in the warmest spirit, and established in the most elevated principles of Christian piety."

Amherst College grew out of a charity school, which was established for the education of indigent young men for the ministerial and the missionary work. It was born of the prayers, and baptized with the tears, of holy men; and, as in the early history of Harvard, the colonists contributed of their deep poverty, "one bringing a piece of cotton stuff, valued at nine shillings; another, a pewter pot of the same value; a third, a fruit-dish, a spoon, and a large and small salt-cellar;" so, in the founding of Amherst College, the friends of learning and religion in the vicinity brought in the materials, and built up the walls with their own hands, while those at a distance gave in money, or the fruit of their labors, whatever they could spare, which might conduce to the endowment of the institution, and the maintenance of its officers and students. Such self-denials and sacrifices, as were made by the founders of these, and, indeed, most of our colleges, could have proceeded only from religious motives, —only from hearts overflowing with love to Christ and his church. Amherst College was one of the *earliest* institutions that grew up under the influence of the foreign missionary enterprise, and the new impulse which was thus given to all benevolent efforts; and it is, in its character and history a type of a new class of colleges which have sprung up, particularly in the new States, and which may be called emphatically, both as regards their origin and influence, Missionary Colleges.

"Western Reserve College was founded by domestic missionaries, and designed to furnish pastors for the infant churches on the Reserve. Illinois College originated in the union of two independent movements; the one emanating from Home Missionary operations in Illinois, the other from a Society of Inquiry respecting Missions at Yale College. The site of Wabash College was dedicated to God in prayer by its founders kneeling upon the snow in the primeval forest. Marietta College was founded mainly to meet demands for competent teachers and ministers of the gospel."

In fact, nearly all of those institutions which have lived and prospered, and exerted a decided influence, even in our literary and political history, were established by evangelical Christians; and have been taught, for the most part, by evangelical ministers, with a direct and special reference to supplying these churches, and the country and the world, with a learned and pious evangelical ministry. Institutions established by worldly men, for mere worldly objects, have not prospered. Infidelity or irreligion, or no religion, may have founded them, but it could not sustain them; and it has been found necessary to transfer them to the hands of religious guardians and teachers, in order to save them from utter extinction. They have been planned by the wisdom of political sages, and fostered by the wealth and power of the State, but they could not be well managed and governed without the sanctions of religion. They have not won the confidence of parents and guardians, for even irreligious parents do not generally want their children educated in infidelity or impiety; and Christianity, though hated in itself, has been welcomed as a necessary means; though excluded by statutes and constitutions, it has, sooner or later, been admitted to a practical and controlling influence. The history of the University of Virginia, the University of South Carolina, Transylvania University, Dickinson College, Girard College, and, to some extent, Harvard College, had we time to give it, would furnish a satisfactory demonstration of these statements. Baptists and Methodists, Congregationalists and Presbyterians,*— all the evangelical Protestant sects, have their prosperous

* Much the larger number by these last-named denominations. Of the 120 colleges in the United States, 13 are Baptist, 13 Methodist and Episcopalian, and the rest, for the most part, under Congregational and Presbyterian influence.

literary institutions in almost every State of the Union; but infidelity has yet to make its first successful enterprise of this sort; and State policy, State patronage, exclusive of religious influence, cannot show a single flourishing college from the Atlantic and the Great Lakes to the Pacific and the Gulf of Mexico.

These are remarkable facts, especially when considered in connection with the voluntary system, and the entire civil and religious liberty of the American people. A wealthy and powerful establishment,—a church wedded to the State, and enriched by State patronage through successive centuries, we might well suppose, could secure such results. A rich and lordly hierarchy, lording it over the consciences and the estates of the whole people, we should think, might build religious colleges by scores in every part of the country, or might subsidize existing literary institutions, and make them subservient to their views of religion. But that the free voluntary movements of so many different denominations of Christians should have reared a hundred and twenty colleges in different parts of these United States,—many of them in the very infancy of the States, or Provinces, and all within little more than two hundred years after the first settlement of the country; and furnished them with such a succession of learned and pious teachers, and brought them so completely under the controlling influence of a practical Christianity,—this is truly remarkable. It shows that Christianity, with all its divisions and corruptions, still possesses a vital energy, and is still guided and guarded by Him who has all wisdom and all power. It shows that the church is still self-denying in her spirit, and far-reaching in her plans; for nothing but self-denying charity, and far-reaching sagacity, will plant colleges in a new country, when there is a present demand for the necessaries of life, rather than for high mental culture. It shows that there is a natural and mutual affinity between religion and learning; that each alternately seeks the alliance and support of the other, while both are left to the freest action and development. It shows that the American people are imbued with a deep, practical conviction that the college was in its origin, and is in its nature, a religious institution; and must be so, if it would realize its proper literary and political ends. Above all, it proves, as we cannot but believe, and would acknowledge with devout gratitude, that the providence of God has watched over our beloved country in all its history, and guarded it against the dangers to which a youthful and free people are most exposed, as if he intended, in spite of adverse agencies, to preserve this goodly land as a heritage for himself.

The college, then, is the daughter of the church, cherished by her with all a mother's love and care, and self-denial. Has the daughter done any thing in return for the mother? Surely she were an unnatural child if she has made no return of filial love and service to her, to whom she owes all that she has, and all that she is, even to her very existence.

Is it nothing to the church that the system of popular education, the preparation of text-books, the examination and direction of teachers, and, to so great an extent, the education of the teachers themselves, is in the hands of men who have been trained by Christian scholars in Christian colleges? Is it a small thing for the church, that colleges established by herself, and conducted by her ablest and best men, give tone, in so great a measure, to the literature of the country, and control the reading of the people, not only in books of history and philosophy, and poetry and belles-lettres, but in those magazines and newspapers, which now occupy more and more the pens of our most thoughtful, learned and elegant writers? Is it of little or no consequence to the church that men educated at Christian colleges have, to so great an extent, filled the office of presidents, and governors, and judges, and other civil magistrates in our country, and are also extending their influence every day more widely among the people through the popularization of learning, and those countless applications of science to common life, which are pouring wealth into the bosom of the church for her enterprises of benevolence? Is it nothing to the church, that so many of our lawyers and physicians, and other men of influence in the community, have been taught in college to recognize the divine origin of Christianity, to respect the institutions of religion, and to carry more or less of Christian principles and a Christian spirit with them into the higher walks of life?

These are some of the indirect contributions of colleges to the church. Now let us look at some more direct returns of revenue which she has received from her investments in colleges. Let us see how well they accomplish the more immediate and more prominent object, which the church contemplated in their establishment.

The ministry of this country has been an educated ministry from the first. The earliest ministers in the colonies were of course educated abroad; but soon there rose up schools of the prophets in the wilderness, and the churches looked, nor looked in vain, to Harvard, and Yale, and Nassau Hall, for pastors to feed them with knowledge and understanding. A minister without a thorough college education would scarcely have been tolerated among the Pilgrim Fathers, or their descendants for a hundred years after them. Sects have since sprung up, that for a time eschewed learning, and listened to rant from the pulpit, while they looked in vain for inspiration. But as they have grown older and wiser, even these sects have fallen in with the spirit of the country and the age, and now they, too, demand a learned, as well as pious ministry; now they yield to none in their zeal and liberality for the establishment of colleges and theological seminaries.

The clerical, far beyond either of the other so-called *learned professions,* is actually composed of men of thorough classical education. Half-educated fledglings are fluttering and tumbling into the practice of law and medicine more frequently now, perhaps, than at any former period of our history. But never before was there a smaller relative proportion of uneducated clergymen; never before was the standard of clerical education and attainment so high, and so imperative on all who would enter the sacred office. . . .

American missions to the heathen had their birth in

a little circle of devoted young men, whose prayers have hallowed the rooms, and the very fields about Williams College, and whose example has blessed the nations in every quarter of the globe. The precise locality where Samuel J. Mills and his associates consecrated themselves to a missionary life, we are happy to learn, has been recently identified, and it is to be purchased and set apart as a perpetual memorial of that sacred epoch in the history of the church. A higher monument would mark this place, were monuments any measure of the importance of the events which they commemorate, than rises from any battlefield in the New or the Old World; and Christians, if they had the spirit of Christ and of Christian missions, would go on pilgrimages, not to Bunker's Hill, or Waterloo, but to "the Haystack," near Williams College. The sacred flame, which first began to burn there, has been kept alive on the same and similar altars. American missionaries have not only been graduates of American colleges, but, with few exceptions, they consecrated themselves to the missionary work, while they dwelt in college walls. Facts show that very few decide to become missionaries after leaving college. "From Dartmouth College have gone out twenty-four missionaries to foreign countries; from Amherst, so recently established, thirty-six; from Williams, thirty-three; from Middlebury, twenty-four." * The colleges stand in a no less sacred relation to the cause of Home Missions. In 1850, Amherst had as many as fifty home missionaries in the field.

The men for all our benevolent enterprises must come from the colleges, and will carry through life very much of the character and spirit they had when in college. Students give more *money* for benevolent objects, in proportion to their means, than almost any other community. This may not be so with all colleges and higher seminaries, but we know it is so in more than one. We have seen the poor student throw his last quarter into the contribution box, saying (with a sublime faith, not perhaps to be imitated by all, but worthy of universal admir-

* Dr. Park's Address before the Western College Society. The number of missionaries from Amherst is now (1854) about 50.

ation), "There is all the money I have in the world. I will have that safe."

But money is the smallest contribution which is made by students in college to the cause of Christian charity. They have first given themselves to the Lord and to his work, wherever and whatever it may be. With a faith, like that of Abraham, they have been willing to leave their country, not knowing whither they go, while with a love, like that of Christ, they have offered up themselves on the altar of reconciliation between God and their fellow-men.

The commencement of the new era of benevolence,— the era of Missionary and Bible, and Tract and Education Societies—was marked by the establishment of an unusual number, we might almost say, a new kind of colleges; and they in turn have sustained and furthered the various forms of associated benevolence, with unwonted zeal and devotion. At the same time (to their honor be it said, as well as in truth and justice), some of the older institutions have caught not a little of the new spirit, and lavished the accumulated treasures of their wisdom and their influence in the support of those moral and religious enterprises which are the glory of the age.

Those revivals of religion, which so illustrate and bless our times, have prevailed in colleges with greater frequency and power than in any other communities; and who can calculate the good influences, direct and indirect, which revivals in colleges have exerted on the churches? How many ministers and magistrates, professional men and men of influence, have *there been born* into the kingdom of Christ; and how many more *re*-converted, so that, like Peter, they could strengthen their brethren? How many, while members of college, have caught the spirit of revivals and of missions, and carried it home to the church to which they belong, and with the characteristic ardor and *strength of young men* in a course of education, diffused it through the place of their nativity? And when such men have been settled in the ministry, their own churches have been revival churches, and missionary churches; the life of the communities around them, and the light of this dark world. It has been estimated that one revival of religion, which took place in Yale College, under the presidency of Dr. Dwight, raised up ministers who were instrumental of the conversion of fifty thousand souls in one generation.

Thus, it appears that marked eras in the history of the church have usually been marked eras in the history of colleges, from the establishment of the first seminary in the early Christian church to the foundation of the last college in our western wilderness. The progress of the churches has been *registered,* so to speak, and their attainments have been secured and perpetuated by the colleges, while, in turn, every new wave of thought, and tide of feeling in the colleges, has had its corresponding wave and tide in the churches. The stream will not permanently rise higher than the fountain. The fountain determines the quality, as well as the height of the stream. The college and the church are alternately or mutually fountain and stream. More frequently the impulse originates in the college. It was so in the Reformation. It was so with the Oxford heresy. The Unitarian defection in New England originated perhaps with the churches, or rather with their pastors, but it has been perpetuated by Harvard College. The tide rose in the churches till it burst open the gates and inundated the college, but now it has turned, and is flowing back, more gradually, but not less powerfully, and even more effectively, from the college into the churches and the community. Let all our colleges become like Harvard, and Unitarianism would overflow the country. Or let them become such schools of infidelity as Jefferson and Girard would fain have established; and, unless they are abandoned and their gates closed, the next generation will forsake the religion of their fathers, and the churches will be deserted by the people. Or let our ministers and men of influence be uneducated, or half educated, and errors and heresies will spring up like thorns and briers in a neglected field; for it is men who are untaught in history (especially the history of doctrines), and undisciplined in their mental and moral faculties, whose minds have been the hot-beds of theological error in every age of the church. To pray for the colleges, then, is to pray for the churches, for an educated and devoted ministry,—for a pure and Protestant Christianity,—for foreign and home missions,—for evangelical revivals of religion; in a word, for churches, that shall live and work, and propagate a sound faith, lively hope and impartial charity through the world.

9.   Francis Wayland: *Thoughts on the Present Collegiate System** (1842)

President Wayland published the following essay in 1842, when he concluded that his efforts to induce the Brown Corporation to broaden the curriculum, establish an elective system, and make faculty salaries dependent on student fees were premature. Though the essay contains many references to his observations in England in 1841, Wayland had no desire to transplant European institutions to America. His reflections on the close ties between Oxford and Cambridge and the leading circles of English society stimulated him to seek some means by which American education might be better adapted to middle-class democracy. Much of his analysis was cast in the dialect of political economy, and he expressed no preference for any one of the several basic institutional reforms which seemed suitable for American colleges.

IMPORTANCE OF THE SUBJECT; ATTEMPTS TO IMPROVE OUR COLLEGIATE SYSTEM

The present system of collegiate instruction is very much the same throughout the United States. With but very

* Francis Wayland, *Thoughts on the Present Collegiate System in the United States* (Boston: Gould, Kendall and Lincoln, 1842), pp. 9–17, 38–41, 108–112, 132–149. On Wayland, see Walter C. Bronson, *The History of Brown University, 1764–1914* (Providence: Published by the University, 1914), Chapters 6–7; and Theodore R. Crane, "Francis Wayland and the Residential College," *Rhode Island History,* XIX, July and October 1960, 65–78, 118–129, and "Francis Wayland: Political Economist as Educator," *Rhode Island History,* XXI, July and October 1962, 65–90, 105–124 (reprinted as *Brown University Papers,* XXXIX, Providence: Brown University Press, 1962).

few exceptions it consists of a four years course, terminating in graduation, all the students pursuing the same
studies, the same labor being required from all, and the
same time being allotted to each. . . . The older institutions have in no important respect ever ventured to
deviate from it, and the new ones have considered their
own organization perfect in just so far as they have been
able to approximate to it.

In connexion with this fact it is proper to remark that
for a very considerable period, a very general opinion
has prevailed that something in the system required material modification.

At one time an attempt was made to supply what was
believed to be a deficiency in the system of collegiate
education by the establishment of Gymnasia or High
Schools. In several instances gentlemen of ripe and varied
learning, with much knowledge of the systems of European education, were induced to connect themselves with
seminaries of this character. Teachers in abundance and
of high reputation were secured, and pupils in great
numbers resorted to them for instruction. But in a few
years these experiments totally failed. Parents were, I
believe, more dissatisfied with them than with the colleges which it was at one time supposed they would
supplant. Next followed Military High Schools, or seminaries for instruction in the higher branches of learning, formed after the model of the U. S. Military Academy at West Point. These very rapidly followed the
course of the Gymnasia; their buildings were deserted,
and I believe that in a few years the establishments themselves generally came under the hammer.

These seminaries were commonly very expensive, and
their advantages were of course confined exclusively to
the children of the wealthy. This was considered by many
persons as the cause of their failure. The next experiment
was varied in this respect, and Manual Labor Schools
were established. The benevolent were called upon to
invest a large amount of property in buildings and land,
with the expectation that students would be able by
their own labor to support themselves, while acquiring a

liberal education. These institutions also flourished, until
the investments had all been consumed, and they then
shared the fate of their predecessors. No one of them,
I believe ever produced at the best more than two or
three per cent. on the principal, so that it would have
been far more economical to have placed the original
capital at ordinary interest, and have bestowed the proceeds upon persons deserving of the charity. The money
thus squandered has not however been wholly thrown
away. It has taught good men to examine somewhat more
carefully into the rationale of schemes of benevolence,
and has served to demonstrate that no man can devote
the time necessary for acquiring a professional education
without the expenditure of money. If he do not pay for
it himself he must by some means or other induce his
neighbors to make the payment for him.

These various modifications in the form of institutions
for education in the higher branches of education having
failed to answer the expectations of the public, nothing
remained but to attempt to improve the colleges themselves. The forms in which this attempt has been made
are various, and they have been attended with various
degrees of success. Some few of them are deserving of a
passing notice.

It has been said that the course of study in our colleges
was formed in a remote age, and that it is adapted only
to a state of society very different from our own. Specially
has it been urged that the study of the *classics* is at best
but useless, that it has no relation to our present duties
and every day engagements, and that the time devoted to
it had much better be employed upon the study of the
Modern Languages. Besides, it has been said that our collegiate course should extend its benefits to merchants,
manufacturers, and every class of citizens. These persons
desire the honors of a degree as much as others. They do
not however wish to waste their time in the study of the
classics, and therefore the studies required of the candidate for a degree should be accommodated so as to meet
these their reasonable wishes. It was predicted that as
soon as this change should be made, our colleges would

be crowded with those who were anxious to avail themselves of these advantages and to obtain the honor of a degree.

In obedience with these suggestions a change was made some years since in the studies of some of our colleges. Both a classical and scientific course were established, the first requiring the study of the Learned and the other substituting in their room the Modern languages. Teachers were engaged, classes were divided, each student had his option, and all who wished were invited to become candidates for a degree upon these modified conditions. But what was the result? No one came to accept of what was thus freely offered. The system dragged for a few years, and then perished from mere inanition.

Very much the same course has been pursued in regard to the higher mathematics. The same objections were made to this branch of a liberal education, and it has been proposed to substitute in their place the study of history or of natural science. To a considerable degree this experiment has been combined with the other, and with very much the same result. The colleges so far as I know, which have obeyed the suggestions of the public, have failed to find themselves sustained by the public. The means which it was supposed would increase the number of students in fact diminished it, and thus things gradually after every variety of trial have generally tended to their original constitution. So much easier is it to discover faults than to amend them; to point out evils than to remove them. And thus have we been taught that the public does not always know what it wants, and that it is not always wise to take it at its word.

But as the number of students in most of our colleges was commonly much less than could be desired, and as colleges have steadily continued to multiply, it was next supposed that the reason why they were not more numerously attended was the high price of tuition. The price of a collegiate education, however, it may be remarked in passing, has always been exceedingly low in this country. It is, and has long been much less than that of private tuition; and the officers of colleges are always

remunerated at a much lower rate than other professional men. Still it was believed that collegiate education
would be in a more prosperous condition if tuition could
be much more nearly given away. When the number of
students in a college began to diminish so that the pit-
tance granted to instructors could no more be doled out,
an effort was next made to raise additional funds for the
support of instructors. This fund has sometimes been
used for the endowment of professorships, and sometimes
for the general reduction of tuition or for the support of
indigent students. Very large sums have been from time
to time appropriated to this purpose. This of course will
partly remedy the evil. When a valuable consideration
is to be given away, it is not generally difficult to find
persons willing to accept of it.

In this manner there is no doubt that a college may
be supported. If after buildings have been erected, and
a considerable amount of funds invested, and the teachers remunerated at the lowest possible rate, pupils cannot be attracted in sufficient numbers to support the
establishment, we may yet be allowed to draw upon the
charities of the public to make up the deficiency, the system may doubtless be sustained. And this is I believe at
present the very general condition of colleges among us.
I doubt whether any one could attract a respectable
number of pupils, however large its endowments and
however great its advantages, did it charge for tuition the
fees which would be requisite to remunerate its officers at
the rate ordinarily received by other professional men. In
some of our colleges education is given away to every
person who enters the plea of indigence. Others are
in possession of funds appropriated to a considerable
amount to this purpose. In most of them, candidates for
the ministry are educated gratuitously or at a great reduction from the ordinary charge for tuition. In this
manner collegiate education has come to be considered
to a very great extent a matter of charity; and the founding of a college consists not so much in providing means
for higher education and thus elevating the general standard of intellectual attainment, as the collecting of funds

for eleemosynary distribution, by which those who desire to pursue the course which we have marked out may be enabled to do so at the least possible cost.

Now I cannot but look at this as an unnatural state of things. Let a man reflect upon the wages of labor in this country, at the ease with which industrious men in every occupation arrive at competence, let him pass through our streets and enter our houses and inspect our modes of living and he will surely say that a very large portion of our people are able to meet the expenses of bestowing upon their children as good an education as they can receive with advantage. There does not appear from our outward circumstances any reason why a man should not pay a fair price for the education of his son just as he pays a fair price for the education of his daughter; or for the furniture, the carpets, the pianos, the mirrors of his parlor, or the implements, the stock, and the acres of his farm. Nor can it be said that as a people we are unaware of the advantages of knowledge. In all our cities and towns, the private instructor is liberally paid. There are certainly all the elements in existence out of which must arise a strong desire for the intellectual improvement of our offspring. And yet while this is the fact we find all around us very large investments made for the purposes of public education, the interest of their investments is bestowed upon the public, and yet we cannot induce men to pursue a collegiate course unless we offer it vastly below its cost, if we do not give it away altogether.

From the preceding facts I think we are warranted in coming to the following conclusions. First, that there is in this country a very general willingness both in the public and on the part of individuals to furnish all the necessary means for the improvement of collegiate education. Second, that the present system of collegiate education does not meet the wants of the public. The evidence of this is seen in the fact that change after change has been suggested in the system without however any decided result, and still more from the fact that although this kind of education is afforded at a lower price than any other, we cannot support our present institutions without giving a large portion of our education away. Third, that this state of things is neither owing to the poverty of our people nor to their indifference to the subject of education. Our citizens seem really more willing to educate other men's sons than their own, to provide the means of education rather than to avail themselves of them after they have been provided. Now, do not these facts indicate the necessity of some change in our educational system. A liberal education is certainly a valuable consideration. Can it not be made to recommend itself; so that he who wishes to obtain it shall also be willing to pay for it? Cannot this general impression in favor of education be turned to some practical account, so that the system may be able to take care of itself? Or at any rate, if after all that has been done we remain without having effected any material change, may it not be well to examine the whole system and see whether its parts may not admit of some better adjustment and work out a more perfect result. . . .

THE PRESENT SYSTEM OF COLLEGIATE INSTRUCTION IN THE UNITED STATES

. . . Oxford and Cambridge form a part, and no unimportant part, of the social system of Great Britain. To these institutions, the youth of the higher classes, from every part of the realm, resort to spend the latter period of their pupilage. There the youthful aristocracy meet and become acquainted with each other. Thither are the eyes of parents from every county in the Kingdom turned with fond anxiety. Thither do the bar, the pulpit, and the senate look for the young men who have there made it known that nature has marked them for distinction. And besides all this, there was never so vast a people bound together by so many and so indissoluble social ties as that of Great Britain. The British Nation, or rather the elite of that nation in a remarkable degree form one great family. London, "that mighty heart," sends out its pulsations to every extremity of the empire, and is in turn receiving from every extremity the life-blood which it vitalizes and sends back again. Every man of distinction is expected to report himself there during some part of the "season," and he must do it in order as Sir Walter Scott says, "to keep himself abreast of society." Hence men of eminence are much more generally known to each other than in any other country that ever existed. And hence the stimulating effect of social opinion is stronger than in any other country upon earth.

Now the Universities live and move and have their being in the very blaze of this social effulgence. Every distinguished man holds, and is proud to hold through life, his connexion with his College and his University. He hears with interest of all that concerns its prosperity. He feels a pride in every pupil of his College or University who has distinguished himself. At the last election of High Steward for the University of Cambridge, gentlemen went from all parts of the Kingdom, merely to give their vote, though public cares obliged them to return the very next hour after they had done it. An instance of this kind came within my own knowledge. Nor is this an uncommon case, but the contrary. Such is the interest which the educated classes in England take in these cherished institutions of learning.

The University thus stands prominently *ante ora omnium*. To obtain rank there, is to place oneself immediately in a position in society; it shows to all, who in their several departments, need the aid of talent, that a man is worth taking up. He becomes a marked man. Something is expected of him and he feels that if he only justifies this expectation, his fortune is made. . . . Now where a position in society is a matter of so much importance as in England, it must at once be seen that the means for obtaining such a position which the Universities afford, must be of incalculable value. And thus when the whole power of the social system is brought to bear upon the University, we can form some conception of the stimulus which it exerts upon the student of high and generous impulses.

Now to all this we have nothing that bears even the shadow of a resemblance. There is in this respect no point of analogy which by any law of association, would lead us to think of the two systems in connexion. In most of our colleges, rank is assigned to the orators at commencement according to scholarship; but even this custom is in danger of passing into desuetude. Some of our institutions, awed by the hoarse growl of popular discontent, have feared that a distinction of this kind savored of aristocracy, and have dropped it like a polluted thing. In but one of our Colleges, to my knowledge, is there any system of premiums for excellence in scholarship. Our community is divided into state sovereignties, and society has here no centre, no heart like London, nor can it ever have. A graduate leaves his College when his course is completed, and his connexion with it and his interest in it cease. We have no centre to which talent of all kinds tends. A class, as soon as it leaves the walls of College, is scattered in a few days to every State and Territory in the union. The College or University forms no integral and necessary part of the social system. It plods on its weary way solitary and in darkness.

Ibant soli sub nocte per umbram.

The Colleges have but little connexion with each other. The public, when strenuously appealed to, does not deny them money. They are interested in education in general and are desirous that the means of education should be afforded to a large class of the community. But here the interest ceases. After men have bestowed money, they seem utterly indifferent as to the manner in which it is to be employed. The educational system has no necessary connexions with any thing else. In no other country is the whole plan for the instruction of the young so entirely dissevered from connexion with the business of subsequent life. At West Point Military Academy, the standing of a young man in his class, determines his place in the army. Every one must see how strong an impulse this connexion must give to diligence and good behavior. Our Colleges suffer greatly from the want of something of this kind.

OF THE DEFECTS OF THE SYSTEM OF COLLEGIATE EDUCATION IN THE UNITED STATES, AND THE MEANS BY WHICH IT MAY BE IMPROVED

. . . There are three modes in which our present system might be modified.

First, the number of studies pursued during the College course, might be limited in such manner that whatever is taught may be taught thoroughly. The College would in this case be open only for persons who are candidates for degrees. The standard of attainment may be as high as is considered desirable. The difference aimed at would be this, that, instead of learning *many* things *imperfectly,* we should learn a *smaller* number of things *well.* I am sure that every man in active life would, on retrospection, wish that his education had been thus conducted. By learning one science well, we learn *how to study,* and how to master a subject. Having made this attainment in one study, we readily apply it to all other studies. We acquire the habit of thoroughness, and carry it to all other matters of inquiry. The course of study at West Point Academy is very limited, but the sciences pursued are carried much farther than in other institutions in our country; and it is owing to this that the reputation of the institution is so deservedly high. The English University course is, in respect to the number of branches pursued, limited, and yet it is remarkably successful in developing the powers of the mind. Observe the maturity and vigor which the young men there frequently obtain. They sometimes go from the University, as for instance, Pitt, Fox, and Canning, directly to the House of Commons, and are competent at once, to take an important part in the labors of that august assembly. And yet more, I apprehend that the acquisition of the habit of thoroughness is the true method of arriving at the most extensive attainments. A few years since I had the pleasure of meeting one of the most learned German scholars who has visited this country. I asked him how it was that his countrymen were able, at so early an age, to obtain the mastership of so many languages. He replied "I began the study of Latin at an early age. Every book that I studied I was made thoroughly acquainted with. I was taught to read and re-read, translate forwards and backwards, trace out every word and know every thing about it. Before I left a book it became as familiar to me as if written in German. *After this I never had any difficulty with any other language.*"

2. But secondly. Suppose a course so limited does not find favor, and it be contended that as the branches of knowledge are multiplied, a greater number must be included in the course of liberal education. If this be thought preferable, let us do this. But let us not attempt impossibilities, nor let us be contented with superficial education. Let us extend the term. It was originally in fact, seven years. Let us make it five, or six. If the requirements of admission were greater, and the College course increased by the addition of one or two years, a great gain would be made to the cause of education. I think that there is but small fear of our doing too much, if we only do it well.

3. The third plan would be to make a College more nearly to resemble a real University; that is, to make it a place of education in all the most important branches of human learning. This might properly include instruction in all professional, as well as ante-professional science. It should comprize teaching in Latin, Greek, French, German, and Hebrew languages, Mathematics, Mechanics, and all the branches of Natural Philosophy, Moral Philosophy, Intellectual Philosophy, Physical Science in all its departments, Rhetoric and its kindred literature, History, as well as instruction in Law and Medicine.

Of these branches, those might be selected which should be required of the candidate for the degree of

Bachelor of Arts, and his graduation might depend not on time of residence, but on proficiency to be determined by examination. Another course embracing other studies might be made requisite to the obtaining of another degree. If one is Bachelor of Arts, the other might be Bachelor of Science, or of Literature. And still more, in order to bring the whole course of study within the scope of University stimulants, the degree of Master of Arts, instead of being conferred without additional attainment, as it is at present, might be conferred only on those who have pursued successfully the whole circle of study marked out for the candidates for both degrees. The degree of Master of Arts would then designate a degree of positive attainment, and would be a valuable and efficient testimonial. As it is now, to all practical purposes, we throw this degree away. It exerts no power of motive whatever. The best and the worst scholars are equally entitled to it on the third year after graduation. It might be made, as it seems to me, to subserve a valuable purpose in a system of education. A still further modification of the studies taught in a College will be suggested on a subsequent page.

It may be a question which of these plans is best suited to the purposes of our country. Either would I think be preferable to our present system. One may answer better in one place and another in another. I merely suggest these as topics for consideration to those who are interested in the cause of Collegiate education. I am desirous at least of laying the case before the visitors and officers of Colleges among us for candid consideration. If they should contribute in even so small a degree to direct the public attention to the points to be aimed at, or even to be avoided, I shall receive a full reward. In this country, if a movement can only be but commenced in the right direction, it will soon make ample progress. I say a movement in the right direction, for I have no idea that any change of value can be made instantaneously. If however the learned and able and self-sacrificing men who are now engaged in the profession of teaching can be led to act wisely and in concert on this subject, and the

public can be brought into harmony with their action, I
believe that a mighty impulse might be communicated to
the cause of education among us.

OF SOME PREVALENT ERRORS IN REGARD
TO COLLEGIATE EDUCATION

. . . The first of these which I shall consider, is the cost
of Collegiate education in this country. It is by many
persons believed to be dear. We are continually re-
minded by all the friends of Colleges that it will never
do to increase our expenses. College education, it is
said, must be cheap, or a College cannot be sustained. If
a new branch of study is to be introduced, or an additional instructor to be appointed, or any improvement is
suggested, we are told to go on by all means, if the
change would be advantageous, only taking care that the
education shall not cost any more. And I think that I
do not greatly mistake in asserting that in the larger
number of instances parents decide upon the institution
to which their sons are to be sent, rather by the cheapness
of the education, than by any other fact in the case. And
hence it is that to most of the annual catalogues of Colleges is appended a statement of expenses including not
only the cost of tuition, board and lodging, but also of
fuel, lights, washing, and I know not how many other
et ceteras. By a comparison of these, a parent or student
can easily learn which is the cheapest College; and as all
lead to the same degree, that is, all confer the right to
attach the same letters to the graduates' name, that which
is the least expensive, has the best prospect of success.

Let us then inquire what is meant when we affirm
that an article is cheap.

If we turn our attention to any article but education,
we can answer the question in a moment. When a
product is brought into the market, and we know the
cost of its creation, and ascertain that the price merely
pays the cost of investment, labor and interest, and yields
to the producer the ordinary rate of remuneration, we

say that it is as cheap as it can be afforded. If it be sold for a less price, the producer must be ruined. If it yield an extravagant remuneration, it is dear, and we know that so long as capital and labor are free, it will be by competition brought down to the average profit of other investments.

And still more, every one is aware that by no possible shrewdness can we permanently keep an article below the cost of its production. We may, if we choose, declare that we will not give more than half the price which we have formerly given. But this will not in any manner alter the case. The producer cannot be induced to give away the half of his product. If it cannot be brought to market at our price, he will cease to produce it and we must do with out it; or else, as is more probable, he will make use of a cheaper and less valuable material, employ less skillful workmen, and produce an article which will afford him a reasonable profit at our arbitrary prices. We get it for a less sum, but we get it no cheaper; we pay a low price for a poor article, and have laid out our money in spite of ourselves at a decided disadvantage.

These principles are exceedingly obvious, and they apply as truly to the case of College Education as to any other. The natural price of such education would be estimated as follows. We should first estimate the amount of capital invested in buildings, libraries, apparatus, and charge upon this sum the ordinary rate of interest. We should add to this, the salaries of professors and other teachers at the rate of remuneration ordinarily earned by persons employed in similar labor. These two items added together, would form the cost of College education; and if nothing more were charged, the article would be furnished at its natural price. It would be cheap just in proportion as the sum charged fell short of these amounts.

What now are the facts in this case? The whole amount invested in grounds, buildings and libraries, is almost actually sunk; that is, it is either given to the public outright, or else it is made to pay but a very small rate of interest. In a College, for instance, with which I am ac-

quainted,* the property of the Institution, in lands,
buildings, &c., is probably worth one hundred and fifty
thousand dollars. The interest of this sum would be nine
thousand dollars per year. The whole amount paid for
the use of it by the students is about eighteen hundred
dollars, or less than two per cent. And it is to be remarked that out of this sum is to be deducted all the
expenses necessary for important repairs. I presume that
the College does not receive for this property much
more than the nett sum of one per cent. This is certainly
as cheap a rate as could be demanded. For the use of this
property and the labors of its professors, the College receives of the students about seven thousand five hundred
dollars. That is, for the use of its buildings and means of
education, together with the labors of eight officers, it
receives fifteen hundred dollars less than it could obtain
from this property alone at the ordinary rate of interest.
In fact were the property to be sold and the purchase
money invested, it could pay a larger salary than at present to its officers, and give away their labors without a
cent of remuneration.

Were this all, it would be sufficient to establish the
truth of what I have asserted. But this is not all. Most
Colleges are in possession of funds to a considerable
amount. In some cases the funds are large. But whether
large or small they are commonly given to the public,
that is they are appropriated either to the support of
indigent students, or else they are applied to the several
purposes of the institution, that is, to the payment of
instructors. In this latter case they reduce the price of
tuition to the whole public to precisely the amount of
their value. In the College to which I have alluded, fifteen hundred dollars annually are appropriated to this
purpose. To how great an extent these remarks apply
to other Colleges I am not competent to say, but I know
that in spirit they apply to all. Whatever means the College may possess are always appropriated upon the same
principle, and with the same design, to reduce, as far
as possible, the price of tuition. I ask any one in the least

* Brown University.—T.R.C.

acquainted with political economy whether there be any thing in the market as cheap as College education.

But this is not all. I have thus far only stated that the investment in College education is almost entirely given to the public. The next item of cost is the salaries of teachers. I will now add that I believe that the instructors of Colleges in this country, are remunerated, at a lower rate than almost any other professional men. I know but very few who are competent to their situation, who might not earn a larger compensation in any other profession. That this is the case, is manifest from the fact that few young men with fair prospects before them can be ever induced to leave their profession for any office that a College can offer. It is my impression that professorships in New England Colleges vary from six hundred to twelve hundred dollars per annum. And I ask, what inducements could such an income offer to a lawyer, physician, or a clergyman, who had only even begun to take rank in his profession. And besides this, it is to be remarked that this salary can very rarely be increased by any efforts of the incumbent. As it is in youth so must he expect it to be in age. It holds out before him the cheerless prospect of circumstances becoming with every year narrower, terminating at last in death which leaves his widow and children, pennyless.

But the officers of Colleges are not only underpaid, if we compare them with men of other professions; they are underpaid if compared with private instructors. In any of our large towns a private instructor who is competent to his place receives a handsome remuneration; a remuneration I presume frequently twice as great as that received by the professors in the nearest College in his vicinity. The price of tuition in a classical day school, in any of our cities is twice or three times as great as that demanded by Colleges. That is, for the labors of six or eight competent men, you pay but half or one third as much as you pay for the labors of one man. In the one case you require the instructor to be responsible for the conduct of the pupil for the whole four years; in the other you require of him attendance only during the

hours of study and assume the other responsibility your-
self. In the one case you have the advantage of a very
large investment almost for nothing, in the other no investment is required except the rent of a convenient
room or two for the purposes of study and recitation. If
this be the case it must appear evident either that the instructors of Colleges are greatly underpaid or else that
they are exceedingly unfit for their offices. But whether
fit or unfit, whether the article which they furnish be
good, bad or indifferent, no one reflecting on these facts
can for a moment doubt of its cheapness. It is, I have no
doubt, afforded to the public at from half to one third of
its cost, while the cost itself is reduced from twenty-five
to fifty per cent. below the ordinary wages of similar
labor.

To a person whose attention has not been attracted to
this subject, all this may seem strange; but I am persuaded that I have not spoken in the language of exag-
geration. I have never conversed on this subject with a
gentleman at all acquainted with active business, who
was not surprised at the low rate of College expenses.
Parents have assured me that they were obliged to send
their sons to College because they could not afford to
bring them up in a good counting house. For the reasons
which I have given, a liberal education for a son, is much
less expensive than a corresponding education for a
daughter. And in a word, it not unfrequently happens
that a young man of industrious and frugal habits, who
enters College, with nothing more than one or two hundred dollars, by laboring in vacations, and sometimes by
devoting an intermediate year to teaching, will graduate
without being in debt, and will in a year or two obtain
a situation more lucrative than that of most of his instructors. Where this is the case I think there can no
complaint be made of the dearness of a Collegiate education. . . .

It is frequently said that this is a republic, here we are
all equal, the avenues to distinction are, and of right
ought to be, open to all; every man whether poor or rich,
of whatever occupation, should have the opportunity of

improving himself to the utmost; this is demanded by the nature of our institutions, and it is important to success in the arts as well as necessary to the full development of the universal mind. To all this I fully agree. It is the expression of my own long cherished sentiments. I would foster these ideas to the utmost of my ability, and I wish that they were universally diffused and universally acted upon. I have here only to remark upon the bearing which they have upon the present question.

1. It is granted that it would be very desirable to establish means, for the improvement in science and the arts, of all classes of the community. I think it desirable that it should be furnished, in many cases, I care not if in all, gratuitously. But I ask if you are about to make a present to your neighbor, is this any reason why you should not pay for it. If you wish to give away education, is this any reason why instructors should not be as well recompensed as other men. It would certainly be an ambiguous charity to oblige your neighbor to furnish you with his goods at half price because you intended to give them away. Or on the other hand, if you really desire to afford the means of improvement to every citizen, is it wise to pay for his instruction so small a price that the education which he receives is worthless; so worthless that he will not receive it as a gratuity. Look at our common school system in New England. Here we offer to all the means of obtaining a common English education. It is all, in some sense, given away. But is this ever considered as a reason why the instructors should be underpaid. And still further; where instructors in our schools have been poorly paid, it has been universally acknowledged to be bad economy; the schools have been badly attended, badly taught, and in ill favor with the public; on the contrary, where instructors have received sufficient remuneration, good men have been without difficulty employed; schools by a change of this kind, have been doubled and almost trebled in numbers, and the system has at once received the favor of the public. If therefore, it be granted that the good of the whole requires the means of education to be open to all, it by no means

follows either that teachers should be underpaid, or that the education should be rendered of but little value, by driving from the profession those who are by talent and discipline, capable of conferring the greatest benefits upon the community.

But let us examine this argument in another point of light. It is asserted that it is important to present to all men in every rank of life the means of full mental development—and therefore, that *Collegiate* education must be reduced to the extremest degree of cheapness. I grant the premises but I deny the conclusion.

If it be desirable to furnish the means of intellectual development to all, and I believe it to be so, then it follows that we should provide the means of this intellectual culture, either by private munificence or public endowment. I know of but one instance in this country in which this has been done, and that is the instance of the Institution in Boston so nobly endowed by the late Mr. Lowell. By the will of that distinguished benefactor of his native city, a provision has been made for the gratuitous delivery of courses of Lectures to the citizens of Boston on the most important branches of Science. The design has been carried out according to the intention of the testator, and with the most triumphant success. The ablest talent of New England, and even of Europe, has been secured for this service, and the lectures have been attended by thronged audiences which have filled one of the largest rooms in the city. The benefit which this charity will confer upon the citizens of Boston in awakening the slumbering intellect, in stimulating the active mind to more zealous inquiry, and in binding together in one, all the different classes of society will be incalculable. And I think I may add that the success of this experiment has arisen in no small degree from the fact that the institution has been conducted on principles analogous to those which I have suggested. Instead of frittering away the means at his disposal by creating a large amount of tolerably good instruction, the gentleman under whose control the bequest has been placed, has determined to render it as valuable as this or any other country could supply. The lecture room has become a centre of universal attraction. How different would have been the result, had courses of inferior lectures been delivered in every school district in the city. No one would have accepted the gift, for no one would have thought it worth his acceptance, and the whole charity would have been a failure.

I say then that granting the importance of providing means of intellectual cultivation for all the community the only inference from the assumption is that such means ought to be provided. I hope the time will come when all our large towns as well as our cities will be thus endowed. But I say that Colleges are not at present such institutions; they are at present *merely schools preparatory to entrance upon some one of the professions.* Whether therefore tuition be cheap or dear, the argument stated above can have no reference to them. Whether it be cheap or dear, the College as at present constituted, can be of no service to those classes of the community referred to in the argument.

I say a College with us is not an establishment for the instruction of any one in whatever he pleases, but for instruction in a particular course, and that in consequence of its forming an isolated society it naturally repels from its association all who are not engaged in similar pursuits. Now this being the case the question at once arises, is there any reason why the public should make a special effort merely to increase the number of professional men. If a man wishes to pursue one profession rather than another, or to change the profession which he has already chosen, he has a perfect right to do so. But is he therefore an object of charity? Are we in special need of recruits to fill the ranks of the professions? Or still more, because he wishes to enter a profession is it desirable in order to accommodate him that we reduce the price of tuition in such a manner as to render the tuition itself of small value not only to him but to all the rest of the community.

But it will doubtless be asked why should not these means of general improvement be connected with Collegiate establishments. Why should not professors in Colleges deliver courses of lectures which would be attractive to the whole community; and why should not the means which are at present available to a part be made available to the whole? I answer at once, I see no reason whatever why it should not be so. I think that such an arrangement would be a great benefit to the officers, the College, and the community. It would open to the instructor a wide and attractive field of professional exertion. It would enlist in favor of the College all the sympathies of the public, and it would spread before the whole people such means for intellectual improvement as the necessities or tastes of each individual might demand.

I am aware that in order to accomplish this result some changes must be effected in our College system, and if this instruction is to be gratuitous, additional professorships must be endowed. The professor must be relieved from much of the police duty which devolves upon him at present. A variety of courses of instruction must be provided for, which do not enter into our present arrangements. But I see no insuperable difficulty in devising a plan which might meet the exigency, specially if such changes should be introduced into our system as I have elsewhere suggested. It is not, however, my intention to enter upon the discussion of this subject. My object is merely to show that the importance of the diffusion of valuable knowledge only teaches us that means for accomplishing so desirable an object should be provided; that it does not apply to Colleges which are merely professional schools; or that if it apply to them at all, it merely goes to prove that they might confer a much wider benefit upon the community were they enabled to modify their present system and greatly enlarge their foundations.

But it will here be asked, what is to be done for our students for the ministry, if the expenses of Colleges are increased. How shall the churches of our land be supplied with pastors. I answer first, if the ministry be adequately supported, and duly sustained, there will be no difficulty in this respect. We shall surely confer no benefit on the ministry by hiring men to enter it, by the promise of an education, and then keeping them in poverty for the rest of their lives. I answer again, this is a question respecting general education, and is therefore to be judged of upon its own merits. If our arrangements for the education of the ministry are at variance with the general advancement of the community, our arrangements must be changed. If we wish to educate a young man for the ministry, there is no reason why we should not pay that price for his education which shall secure the best instruction both to him and to every one else. To do otherwise would be to inflict an injury both upon ourselves and upon the public. In a word, when we are deliberating upon a plan for the intellectual improvement of the whole community, let us keep that object simply and steadily in view, and we may be assured that if the good of the whole be promoted the good of the part cannot be neglected. . . .

In answer to all that I have said, I am perfectly aware that it may be urged that I am recommending dear instead of cheap education; that I wish to restrict the number of educated men; and that all this is at variance with the nature of our institutions. To the suggestion I can only reply that I can conceive of no motive which should induce an American citizen either to entertain or to promulgate such an opinion. As to the charge of wishing to render education dear, I reply in the first place that nothing that I have said is, so far as I know, chargable with this inference. It has been commonly taken for granted that our *first* and most important business is to make education *cheap*. This assumption I have denied and on the contrary have asserted that our most important business is to make it *good;* that its *goodness* is our *first* concern, and its cheapness only secondary; and that by seeking first of all to render it cheap we were in danger of rendering it useless.

But this is not all, I have endeavored to show that by multiplying Colleges, and spending so large an amount of our funds in buildings, we have rendered our means for the reduction of the price of tuition almost useless. I also believe that another system might be adopted which by attracting a greater number of students, and stimulating teachers to greater energy and efficiency, would attract higher talent to the professional chair; without in the least increasing the expenses of each individual pupil. What I propose then in this respect, may be briefly summed up as follows: Let the education in our Colleges and Universities be exact, generous and thorough; let it be rendered capable of improvement, and let it be for the interest of all connected it with [with it] to improve it, whether it cost more or less than at present; And secondly let it be rendered as cheap as is consistent with goodness; and still more, let provision be made either in connexion with Colleges or independently of them, for the wide dissemination of knowledge in science and the arts; and let this knowledge be of the very best description which American scholarship can supply. Such are in few words my sentiments on this subject, and I hope that I have not uttered any thing at variance with them.

I close this chapter with one other remark; it is upon the commonly received notion that a course of education must be popular. If by being popular it is meant that it must follow every whim of the day, and introduce or discard studies because for the time being they may be in vogue or out of it; if it be meant that our course of discipline must change at the will of every popular convention which may endorse the theoretical notions of an educational reformer, I must be permitted to live a little longer in doubt of the assertion. If it however be meant that it must commend itself to the good sense and patriotism of the American people, I assent to it most cordially. Nothing which is not popular in this sense can be or ought to be sustained. But in order to secure this kind of popularity, we must strive to render education good. We must adopt our plans not only for the present but for the future; we must honestly strive to render our whole course of higher education as valuable and as universally available as possible. We must not only do this but we must spread before the public our reasons for so doing and explain the manner in which we intend to accomplish it. I do most honestly believe that by so doing we shall carry the whole community with us. If we would be popular let us remember that we can never attain our end by aiming at it directly. The approbation of our fellow citizens will in the end be conferred not on those who desire to please them, but on those, who honestly do them good. Popularity is valuable when it follows us, not when we run after it; and he is most sure of attaining it, who, caring nothing about it, honestly and in simplicity, and kindness earnestly labors to render his fellow men wiser, and happier, and better.

Francis Wayland: *Report to the Corporation of Brown University** (1850)

Eight years after the publication of his Thoughts on the Present Collegiate System, *Wayland's tone was different, but his institutional objectives were not yet fully clarified. Assured at last of Corporation support for long-cherished reforms, he abandoned his earlier diffidence in a manifesto to the nation which reflected his intense dedication to moral principle and elaborated in a hastily conceived program of reforms the convictions about educational policy and purpose that he had developed during the previous three decades. He felt little veneration for traditional features of the college system, as is indicated by his willingness to modify established degrees, which most American educators considered essential certificates of academic integrity.*

* Francis Wayland, *Report to the Corporation of Brown University, on Changes in the System of Collegiate Instruction, Read March 28, 1850* (Providence: George H. Whitney, 1850), pp. 50–61, 72–75.

. . . If it be the fact that our colleges cannot sustain themselves, but are obliged to make repeated calls upon the benevolence of the community, not because the community is poor and education inordinately expensive, but because, instead of attempting to furnish scientific and literary instruction to every class of our people, they have furnished it only to a single class, and that by far the least numerous; if they are furnishing an education for which there is no remunerative, but even at the present low prices, a decreasing demand; if they are, not by intention, but practically, excluding the vastly larger portion of the community from advantages in which they would willingly participate, and are thus accomplishing but a fraction of the good which is manifestly within their power, then it would seem that relief must be expected from a radical change of the system of collegiate instruction. We must carefully survey the wants of the various classes of the community in our own vicinity, and adapt our courses of instruction, not for the benefit of one class, but for the benefit of all classes. The demand for general education in our country is pressing and universal. The want of that science, which alone can lay the foundation of eminent success in the useful arts, is extensively felt. The proportion of our young men who are devoting themselves to the productive professions, is great and annually increasing. They all need such an education as our colleges, with some modifications in their present system, could very easily supply. Is there not reason to believe that, if such an education were furnished, they would cheerfully avail themselves of it?

Were an institution established with the intention of adapting its instruction to the wants of the whole community, its arrangements would be made in harmony with the following principles.

1. The present system of adjusting collegiate study to a fixed term of four years, or to any other term, must be abandoned, and every student be allowed, within limits to be determined by statute, to carry on,

at the same time, a greater or less number of courses as he may choose.

2. The time allotted to each particular course of instruction would be determined by the nature of the course itself, and not by its supposed relation to the wants of any particular profession.

3. The various courses should be so arranged, that, in so far as it is practicable, every student might study what he chose, all that he chose, and nothing but what he chose. The Faculty, however, at the request of a parent or guardian, should have authority to assign to any student, such courses as they might deem for his advantage.

4. Every course of instruction, after it has been commenced, should be continued without interruption until it is completed.

5. In addition to the present courses of instruction, such should be established as the wants of the various classes of the community require.

6. Every student attending any particular course, should be at liberty to attend any other that he may desire.

7. It would be required that no student be admitted as a candidate for a degree, unless he had honorably sustained his examination in such studies as may be ordained by the corporation; but no student would be under any obligation to proceed to a degree, unless he chose.

8. Every student would be entitled to a certificate of such proficiency as he may have made in every course that he has pursued.

The courses of instruction to be pursued in this institution might be as follows:

1. A course of instruction in Latin, occupying two years.
2.   "   "   in Greek,   "   "
3.   "   "   in three Modern Languages.
4.   "   "   in Pure Mathematics, two years.
5.   "   "   in Mechanics, Optics, and Astronomy, either with or without Mathematical Demonstrations, $1\frac{1}{2}$ years.

6. A course of instruction in Chemistry, Physiology and Geology, 1½ years.
7. A course of instruction in the English Language and Rhetoric, one year.
8. A course of instruction in Moral and Intellectual Philosophy, one year.
9. A course of instruction in Political Economy, one term.
10.   "   "   in History, one term.
11.   "   "   in the Science of Teaching.
12.   "   "   on the Principles of Agriculture.
13.   "   "   on the Application of Chemistry to the Arts.
14.   "   "   on the Application of Science to the Arts.
15.   "   "   in the Science of Law.

Some of these courses would require a lesson or lecture every working day of the week, others only two or three in the week. Any professor might be allowed to conduct the studies of more than one course, if he could do it with advantage to the institution.

Should this idea be adopted, and the instruction given in this college be arranged on these principles, it would be seen that opportunity would be afforded to modify it as experience should prove desirable. Some courses may be abridged or abolished, and others added or extended. The object of the change would be to adapt the institution to the wants, not of a class, but of the whole community. It by no means is to be taken for granted, in a country like our own, that every college is to teach the same studies, and to the same extent. It would be far better that each should consult the wants of its own locality, and do that best, for which it possessed the greatest facilities. Here would arise opportunity for diversified forms of excellence; the knowledge most wanted would the more easily become diffused, and the general progress of science would receive an important impulse from every institution of learning in our land.

It may be proper here to indicate the manner in which, as your committee believes, the plan proposed would relieve the embarrassments of the institution.

In explaining their views on this part of the subject, it is not pretended, that with any plan that can be devised, in the present condition of New England, this can be wholly a self-supporting institution. Education is afforded at all our colleges so far below cost, that, at cost price, it is doubtful whether it could be disposed of. The college is far from supporting itself now. Unless it receives some aid, it cannot be carried on. The inquiry which we have felt it to be our duty to make, has been this: In what manner, at the least expense to its friends, can it be put in a condition to support itself? It has seemed to your committee, that in no other way can this result be arrived at, than by extending its advantages to every class of the community, and thus increasing the number of its pupils. The more it can do for itself, the less need its friends do for it.

That such a change as is here proposed, would add to the number of its pupils, seems to your committee probable, for several reasons.

1. The course of instruction will, it is hoped, present a better preparation for the learned professions, than that pursued at present. There is no reason, therefore, why this class of pupils should be diminished.

2. Opportunity would be afforded to those who wished to pursue a more generous course of professional education, to remain in college profitably for five or six years, instead of four, as at present.

3. Many young men who intend to enter the professions, are unwilling or unable to spend four years in the preparatory studies of college. They would, however, cheerfully spend one or two years in such study, if they were allowed to select such branches of science as they chose. This class would probably form an important addition to our numbers, and we should thus, in some degree, improve the education of a large portion of all the professions.

4. If we except the ancient languages, there are but few of the studies now pursued in college, which, if well taught, would not be attractive to young men pre-

paring for any of the active departments of life. If these several courses were so arranged as to be easily accessible to intelligent young men of all classes, it may reasonably be expected that many will desire to spend a term, a year, or two years, under our instruction.

5. It is not probable that the courses of instruction in agriculture, or chemistry, or science applied to the arts, will, of necessity, occupy all the time of the student. Many of these persons will probably desire to avail themselves of the advantages so easily placed in their power. Another source of demand for the courses in general science would thus be created.

Should these expectations be realized, it will be perceived that the addition to our numbers will come from classes who now receive no benefit whatever from the college system, as it at present exists. Our numbers would thus be increased without diminishing the number of students in other colleges in New England; and we should be carrying the blessings of scientific and literary education to portions of society from which they have thus far been practically excluded.

Perhaps it may not be inappropriate to add, that if the above views be correct, any college in our country now able to support itself, might easily adopt, to a considerable extent, the system we have ventured to recommend. Its means now are, its funds and its fees for tuition. It is not supposed that the number of its students could be diminished by offering its advantages to vastly larger classes of the community. Supposing its numbers to be the same, it would have the same means of support as at present. There would seem, therefore, to be no particular risk in trying the experiment, since its resources will be increased by every student that it may attract from those classes of society that now yield it no income.

If reasons need be offered for attempting the changes in our collegiate system that have been here indicated, the following will readily suggest themselves.

1. IT IS JUST.—Every man who is willing to pay for them, has a right to all the means which other men enjoy, for cultivating his mind by discipline, and enriching it with science. It is therefore unjust, either practically or theoretically, to restrict the means of this cultivation and discipline to one class, and that the smallest class in the community.

If every man who is willing to pay for them, has an *equal* right to the benefits of education, every man has a *special* right to that *kind* of education which will be of the greatest value to him in the prosecution of useful industry. It is therefore eminently unjust, practically to exclude the largest classes of the community from an opportunity of acquiring that knowledge, the possession of which is of inestimable importance, both to national progress and individual success. And yet we have in this country, one hundred and twenty colleges, forty-two theological seminaries, and forty-seven law schools, and we have not a single institution designed to furnish the agriculturist, the manufacturer, the mechanic, or the merchant with the education that will prepare him for the profession to which his life is to be devoted.

Our institutions of learning have generally been endowed by the wealth of the productive classes of society. It is surely unjust that a system should be universally adopted, which, practically, excludes them from the benefits which they have conferred upon others.

2. IT IS EXPEDIENT.—The moral conditions being equal, the progress of a nation in wealth, happiness, and refinement, is measured by the universality of its knowledge of the laws of nature, and its skill in adapting these laws to the purposes of man. Civilization is advancing, and it can only advance in the line of the useful arts. It is, therefore, of the greatest national importance to spread broadcast over the community, that knowledge, by which alone the useful arts can be multiplied and perfected. Every producer, who labors in his art scientifically, is the best of all experi-

menters; and he is, of all men, the most likely, by discovery, to add to our knowledge of the laws of nature. He is, also, specially the individual most likely to invent the means by which those laws shall be subjected to the service of man. Of the truth of these remarks, every one must be convinced, who will observe the success to which any artisan arrives, who, fortunately, by his own efforts, (for at present he could do it in no other way,) has attained to a knowledge of the principles which govern the process in which he is employed.

Suppose that, since the Revolution, as much capital and talent had been employed in diffusing among all classes of society, the knowledge of which every class stands in need, as has been employed in inculcating the knowledge needed in preparation for the professions, is it possible to estimate the benefits which would have been conferred upon our country? The untold millions that have been wasted by ignorance, would have been now actively employed in production. A knowledge universally diffused of the laws of vegetation, might have doubled our annual agricultural products. Probably no country on earth can boast of as intelligent a class of mechanics and manufacturers, as our own. Had a knowledge of principles been generally diffused among them, we should already have outstripped Europe in all those arts which increase the comforts, or multiply the refinements of human life. Perhaps, in the earlier history of our country, such knowledge would not have been adequately appreciated. That period, however, has now passed away. An impulse has been given to common school education, which cannot but render every man definitely sensible of his wants, and consequently eager to supply them. The time then would seem to have arrived, when our institutions of learning are called upon to place themselves in harmony with the advanced and rapidly advancing condition of society.

3. IT IS NECESSARY.—To us, it seems that but little

option is left to the colleges in this matter. Any one who will observe the progress which, within the last thirty years, has been made by the productive classes of society, in power, wealth, and influence, must be convinced that a system of education, practically restricted to a class vastly smaller, and rapidly decreasing in influence, cannot possibly continue. Within a few years, the manufacturing interest has wrung the corn laws from the aristocracy of Great Britain. Let any one recall the relative position of the professions, and of the mercantile and manufacturing interests, in any of our cities, twenty years since, and compare it with their relative position now, and he cannot but be convinced, that a great and a progressive change has taken place. Men who do not design to educate their sons for the professions, are capable of determining upon the kind of instruction which they need. If the colleges will not furnish it, they are able to provide it themselves; and they will provide it. In New York and Massachusetts, incipient measures have been taken for establishing agricultural colleges. The bill before the legislature of New York, provides for instruction in all the branches taught in our colleges, with the exception of languages. It is to be, in fact, an institution for giving all the education which we now give, agricultural science being substituted for Latin and Greek. What is proposed to be done for the farmers, must soon be done either for or by the manufacturers and merchants. In this manner, each productive department will have its own school, in which its own particular branch of knowledge will be taught, besides the other ordinary studies of a liberal education. A large portion of the instruction communicated will thus be the same in all. Mathematics, Mechanics, Chemistry, Physiology, Rhetoric, Moral and Intellectual Philosophy, and Political Economy, will be taught in them all. The colleges teach precisely the same sciences, with the addition of Latin and Greek, in the place of the knowledge designed in these separate schools, for a particular profession.

If the *prestige* of colleges should be thus destroyed, and it be found that as good an education as they furnish, can be obtained in any of those other schools, the number of their students will be seriously diminished. If, by this dissemination of science among all the other classes of society, the tendency towards the professions should be still farther arrested, the colleges will be deserted by yet larger numbers. They may become very good foundations for the support of instructors, but very few will be found to avail themselves of their instructions.

Is not such a result as this to be deplored? Is it desirable that so many teachers should be employed in teaching precisely the same things? All the branches of general science, taught in any one generous school, must be taught in them all. The colleges already have existing arrangements for teaching them. They are, to a considerable extent, supplied with libraries, apparatus, and all the means of instruction. Would it not seem desirable, that they should so far modify their system, as to furnish all the instruction needed by the various classes of society, who desire special professional teaching, and so arrange their courses of general knowledge, that all, of every class, may, with equal facility, avail themselves of their advantages? In this manner the colleges will reap all the benefit arising from the diffusion and progress of knowledge. Pursuing any other course, they would seem to suffer injury from one of the most hopeful indications of the progress of civilization.

. . . In general, it may be taken for granted, that unless a young man be remarkably dull or incorrigibly negligent, if he enters college and pursues the prescribed course to its close, he will be admitted to the degree of A. B. The diversity of attainment is not, perhaps, as great as may be found in the British universities; we make none so good scholars, we graduate few quite so destitute of scholarship; but our range is certainly great enough to show a wide departure from the statutory provisions.

If we should ask, what, among all these conflicting precedents, comes the nearest to a general requirement, we must answer, that it is a residence of four years, and the payment of the college bills. This seems to be demanded in all cases, while the amount of statutory and of practical requirement is as great as can easily be imagined. Degrees are given to candidates of almost every grade of attainment, but never unless the student has made out a given term of residence, and paid the requisite fees.

Amidst this conflict of precedents and principles, what shall we do? Shall we follow the example of Oxford, and give degrees simply for attainments in the classics; or of Cambridge, and confer them for excellence in the mathematics? Or shall we adopt the curriculum of the Scottish Universities, which approaches nearer to our own? Or shall we continue to require examinations in twice or thrice as many studies as any other universities in the civilized world? To either of these courses substantial objections could be urged.

If any equitable rule could be applied to this case, it would be this, that a degree of A. B. should signify the possession of a certain amount of knowledge, and A. M. of a certain other amount in addition. But what shall this amount be? If we mean that our instruction shall be exact, and adapted to the purposes of mental discipline, the number of studies must be reduced. Suppose, then, we select those that shall designate the amount of knowledge required in a candidate for a degree. This, however, will form but a portion of the studies taught in the university. There may be other branches of knowledge out of this course, as valuable, and as truly knowledge, as those included within it. Some of those not in the first course may be substituted for those within it. By adopting in this manner a system of equivalents, we may confer degrees upon a given amount of knowledge, though the kind of knowledge which makes up this amount may differ in different instances. Thus, for instance, suppose a course should be prescribed, containing a given amount of Latin, Greek, Mathematics, and

Natural and Moral and Intellectual Philosophy, and
Rhetoric, as the basis of requirement for degrees. In determining upon equivalent courses, a certain amount of
some other study might compensate for Latin, or Greek,
as a certain amount of some other study might be a compensation for the higher mathematics, or intellectual
philosophy, and so of the rest. An arrangement of this
kind would seem just, and to us it seems not to be impracticable.

The objection that would arise to this plan, would
probably be its effect upon the classics. It will be said,
that we should thus diminish the amount of study bestowed on Latin and Greek. To this the reply is easy. If
by placing Latin and Greek upon their own merits, they
are unable to retain their present place in the education
of civilized and Christianized man, then let them give
place to something better. They have, by right, no pre-
ëminence over other studies, and it is absurd to claim
it for them. But we go further. In our present system we
devote some six or seven years to the compulsory study of
the classics. Besides innumerable academies, we have one
hundred and twenty colleges, in which, for a large part
of the time, classical studies occupy the labors of the student. And what is the fruit? How many of these students
read either classical Greek or Latin after they leave college? If, with all this labor, we fail to imbue our young
men with a love for the classics, is there any reason to
fear that any change will render their position less advantageous? Is there not reason to hope, that by rendering this study less compulsory, and allowing those who
have a taste for it to devote themselves more thoroughly
to classical reading, we shall raise it from its present de-
pression, and derive from it all the benefit which it is
able to confer?

10.   Henry Philip Tappan:
Inaugural Discourse*
(1852)

President Tappan's hopes were never more sanguine nor his style more felicitous than in his first official appearance at the University of Michigan. The philosophical basis of his educational thought and his admiration for Prussian models are evident in this address, which incorporates essential portions of his treatise on University Education *(1851).*

There is a higher law of our being which commands us to thought, duty, and immortality. The very stretch of our material prosperity shows this higher law in the skill, fore-cast, and energy which are implied—shows what capacities we possess, and reminds us of the possibilities of nobler gifts and of diviner destinies. We can think; but, beyond mere utility, there are science, taste, art, patriotism, morality, religion to be thought out. We can im-

* A Discourse, Delivered by Henry P. Tappan, D.D. at Ann Arbor, Mich., on the occasion of His Inauguration as Chancellor of the University of Michigan, December 21st, 1852 (Detroit: Advertiser Power Presses, 1852), pp. 5–9, 16–28, 31–32, 40–46. Tappan's University Education (New York: George P. Putnam, 1851) should be read entire; excerpts are in Richard Hofstadter and Wilson Smith, eds., American Higher Education: A Documentary History (Chicago: University of Chicago Press, 1961), Vol. II, pp. 488–511; also included in this volume (pp. 515–545) is his talk, The University; Its Constitution, and Its Relations, Political and Religious, a response in 1858 to the opponents of his ambitious plans for the University of Michigan. On Tappan, see Charles M. Perry, Henry Philip Tappan, Philosopher and University President (Ann Arbor: University of Michigan Press, 1933).

prove and create; but, there is an intellectual and spiritual nature to be improved, as well as industrial skill; and there are works of beauty, and institutions of learning and religion to be created, as well as steamboats, railroads, trade and manufactures. The human being may not expend himself upon the outward prosperities of the world which he inhabits; he has a higher and more important work to do for his own nature. His, is not a life of work and play intermingled; but, a life of work and self education intermingled: not a life of success and enjoyment, and then to end life and just to die; but a life of discipline, of growing wise and good, and of diffusing wisdom and goodness, and in dying still to live in institutions that go on from generation to generation to exert a power to make men wise and good—and still to live in the grateful and pleasant memories of those who in the past recall the fathers of the present, and find in the burning and shining light of an imperishable example the guide of duty, and the stimulus of hope.

Institutions of learning have been founded both by individuals and the State. The Universities of Oxford and Cambridge, and the University of Paris were the work of individual munificence and enterprise in their inception, and in much of their after development. So, also, most of the Colleges of our country have been created by individuals. The State lent its aid when these institutions had already attained conspicuity, and given demonstrations of their value and importance. Prussia and Michigan are examples of States creating Educational Systems. The first has been completely successful, and the institutions of Prussia, like ancient learning and art, stand before us as models which we are constrained to admire, to approve and to copy. The institutions of Michigan are yet in their infancy, but we think there is the promise of a bright career, of a full and ripe development, which cannot well disappoint us. . . .

In our country where property changes hands so rapidly, and where the most solidly built estates must finally go to heirs we know not whom, and be melted again into the multitudinous channels of trade, how important that we, the men of to-day, who hold the wealth and the power, should, while our day lasts, build obelisks and pyramids which shall stand when all things else have been swept away! We cannot entail estates in our country to our legal heirs. But an estate might be entailed in a great University as long as our country shall exist—a splendid beneficence—a monument worthy of the ambition of any man, or of any number of men who would lay the foundation and the corner stones thereof. And even in countries where estates can be entailed, how many fair baronies and earldoms have perished in the wrecks of time, while the endowments of Eton and Winchester, of Oxford and Cambridge, of the Bodleian library remain, handing down the names of their founders to a grateful posterity, quickening ever the intellectual, moral and social life of England, nurturing great men, fostering universal knowledge, enriching the fields of literature, and making the name of England glorious to the end of time!

In a commercial community, commercial modes of thinking will prevail more or less even in undertakings which are not intrinsically of a commercial character. It is well, therefore, to look at the establishment of institutions of learning in a commercial point of view, also. Literature, Science, Arts, educational apparatus, and labor, all increase the commodities of trade, and add to national wealth. What a vast amount of capital is enlisted in the book trade and in newspapers! Think of the manufacture of paper and types, of cloth and leather for binding, of gold leaf and other ornaments; think of the multitude of laborers employed in printing establishments, binderies, and publishing houses. All this is set agoing by the thoughts of solitary men—by men whom literary institutions, directly, or indirectly, furnish with ideas, and permeate with the spirit of authorship. Every new book is a new commodity of trade. There is so much added not merely to entertainment and culture, but also to the stock of industry, and the sources of wealth. Suppose that all the books which have been made by men who have been trained directly by Universities, or who have lived in countries where they have shed their light, were at once removed from trade, would it not be like the destruction of the cotton, or sugar, or tobacco, or tea and coffee trade? And a good book is an everlasting commodity: Homer, Milton, Shakspeare, Byron, Scott, Euclid, Bacon, Bunyan, and all like these—have they not given to trade commodities which can never perish? Are not Webster's dictionary and spelling book durable commodities? Who can calculate the industry which has been employed, the wealth that has been, and is still to be created by the publication of even one of these books? The same remarks are plainly applicable to painting, sculpture, music and all those arts which adorn human life: they create valuable stocks in trade, and furnish all those embellishments which are deemed essential in the manufacture of useful fabrics.

Without astronomy there would be no navigation across oceans, and hence no distant commerce. Without mechanicians and engineers, there would be no steam engines and railroads. Without chemistry, there would be no improvements in agriculture and manufactures.

In demanding the highest institutions of learning, therefore, we demand that, which by giving the highest advantages to literary and scientific pursuits, brings into being, most abundantly, books, fine arts, mechanical inventions, and improvements in the useful arts; thus creating not only, important and indispensable commodities in trade, but providing also, the very springs of all industry and trade, of all civilization and human improvement, of all national wealth power and greatness.

A people aiming at large increase of wealth by agriculture, manufactures, and commerce, of all others should aim to found and foster the noblest institutions of learning. On their own principles they should do so. They of all others require men of science.

A great University, too, in any place, by its direct expenditures, by the numbers which it brings together, by the industry which it calls into action in its necessary going on, is an important element of commercial prosperity, besides all the collateral and consequential commercial benefits which we have above shown to be so vast and vital. The city of Edinburgh is a city of one hundred and fifty thousand inhabitants. Its University is the foundation of all its prosperity. Take that away, and it would sink into comparative insignificance. New Haven in our own country affords another illustration of the same kind.

But all these considerations are to be named, only, to meet every kind of objection, and to demonstrate how every form of good must attend upon institutions which some would appreciate only in these lower points of view. There can be no doubt of the truth of the principle, that to pursue those ends which are demanded by the highest and holiest part of our being, will involve our best interests in every relation in which we are placed; a principle announced by the Divine Teacher when he said, "Seek first the kingdom of God and his righteousness, and all these things will be added unto you," and so that what conduces most to the intellectual and moral culture of society, will likewise make wealth and prosperity to abound. But, nevertheless, in arguing a great cause we shall choose to place it upon that empyreal height of reason, truth and duty, which is its native dwelling place. And thus we say to individuals, and to the State, let us create the highest and best institutions of learning at whatever cost, that those who would learn, and those who would advance human knowledge, may want nothing that can aid them. Let us stand up before the world with our good and great things, as well as with our useful and prosperous things. Let us make men as well as houses and railroads. Let us have eternal thoughts circulating among us as well as gold and silver. . . .

A University is the highest possible form of an institution of learning. Whatever schools exist, less than this must be incomplete without it. It embraces when fully developed, as its very name indicates, all possible means for studying every branch of knowledge, and thus perfecting education; and all possible means for making new investigations, and thus advancing knowledge.

It is evident, at once, that every nation ought to possess

such institutions. Does not every nation require for its independent civilization, for its intellectual power and glory, for the purposes alike of its culture, its arts, and its commerce, to possess within itself the means of gaining all knowledge, and the means of advancing all knowledge?

Again it is evident that to no nation under heaven can such institutions be more important than to the United States. We have made ourselves well nigh independent of other nations in all the forms of productive industry; Must we still remain dependent upon the scholars and artists of other nations? We have reached a high political and commercial developement; do we not need a corresponding intellectual, artistic, and social developement to attain the moral forces, the refined graces, and the healthful balance of society? Nay can we truly be called a nation, if we cannot possess within ourselves the sources of a literary, scientific, and artistic life as well as of a political and commercial?

To form a proper idea of what is contemplated in the organization of a University, it is necessary to take into view the range of human knowledge itself. Let us, briefly, represent this:

All knowledge must be a knowledge of every thing standing around men, and objective to him, or, a knowledge of man himself—the being that knows.

I. A knowledge of that which is objective to man. Here is, first of all, pure space conceived of as void of entity.— Then in this pure space we draw lines, and conceive of and represent relations, and thus create an absolute and pure science—the science of Geometry. And we who are active in this do, necessarily, become conscious of succession—the succession of our own thoughts, so this succession in the speculative activity of our minds, becomes the condition of another pure science—of Analysis related to time as Geometry is to space.

Next, we look at that which occupies time and space. And here we have, in the first place, the great planetary masses which compose the universe, viewed, merely, as to form, magnitude, gravity, and motion.

These masses being defined in space and having their motion measured in time, the pure sciences of space and time are applied to determine their laws: and thus we arrive at Astronomy.

There is but one of these masses that we are immediately connected with—our own earth. When we come to examine it, we find it, generally to consist of solid, fluid, and—the atmosphere being a part of it—aeriform substances. These determined under conceptions of gravity, motion, and force, constitute General Physics.

The light, by which we see all things, moving in straight lines is reduced to a distinct and peculiar science; and Optics become an illuminated Geometry.

We next proceed to examine the solid earth more particularly; and finding it to consist of distinct substances having remarkable differences, we classify them, and construct the science of Mineralogy.

Then we look at the crust of the earth, generally, and we find it broken up, and thrown into a great variety of positions forming hill, mountain, and valley: and here observing that the different minerals are presented in aggregate masses, and arranged in a certain order of stratification, indicating successive and mighty revolutions, we are led to the science of Geology.

But, the substances around us are continually undergoing changes which appear to be connected with heat, moisture, air, and light. We cannot forbear to pry into these changes, especially, as they are connected with our own sustenance, health, and comfort. In making these investigations, we experiment upon the combinations of substances; and step by step, we find out laws of composition and decomposition, until, earth, air, and water are resolved into their simple elements: and now we have the science of Chemistry.

But, in carrying on investigation and experiment, we become acquainted with new forces in nature: we are no longer confined to the centripetal and centrifugal forces —we have also, Galvanism, Electricity, Magnetism, and Elasticity or Expansion.

We have not yet done with the substances around us.

They are presented to us, not merely as aggregations of like substances, or as compositions of unlike, they are presented, also, under the law of that mysterious force which we call Life. Our investigations into the phenomena of life lead us to the general science of Biology. Under this we have Animal and Vegetable Physiology, branching out again into Zoology and Botany. The fossil remains of the earth connect Biology with Geology. The historic indications of Geology connect it with Astronomy.

In forming our acquaintance with nature, we have become conscious of two commanding ideas—Utility and Beauty. The world is useful: the world is beautiful. But the knowledge we have gained by experience enables us, under the light of these ideas, to conceive of other forms of utility and beauty besides those which are presented in the rude uncultivated nature around us. Then comes the application of our skill and industry. The forests are leveled; the fields are cultivated; human habitations are built; a wonderful variety of fabrics are produced for comfort and elegance; vessels cover the rivers, lakes and oceans; roads, bridges, canals, railroads, form artificial avenues of communication across continents. We now have Agriculture, Manufactures, Mechanical Arts and Commerce; and Wealth as their combined result—all growing out of our knowledges. The activity of human thought—scientific cultivation has done it all.

Again, the idea of beauty, in the presence of the beautiful in nature, leads to conceptions of proportion of harmony, symmetry and grace; and man becomes the Artist of the beautiful in Architecture, Gardening, Sculpture, Painting, Poetry and Music. Scientific knowledge and Mechanical skill united with the idea and taste of beauty, throw over human society the charms of a purer and more elevated existence.

II. Let us now turn to man himself—the being who knows. Of all that is going on in his own mind, man is conscious. There is a world of phenomena within him, as well as without him. All men are, more or less, observant of these phenomena, just as they are more or less observant of the phenomena without. But, as only studied and methodical observation, without, leads to physical science; so, also, only studied and methodical observation, within, leads to metaphysical science, or philosophy. It is by this profound reflection that pure philosophy, comprehending Ontology, Psychology, Aesthetics, Logic, and Morals, is developed. And philosophy throws its light over all human thought, and activity, unfolding the principles of law and government, determining the methods of reasoning and investigation, defining the scope of the understanding, and settling all ultimate principles.

But with this study of man within—of man the universal, must be joined the study of all that man has done on the great theatre of the world, appearing in nations and individuals. Hence arises History under its multifarious divisions, embracing all human action, all human progress.

With this, there is, necessarily connected the study of languages, literature, art, antiquities, law, religion, ethnology and geography.

Now when we speak of a University, we speak of an institution that shall make adequate provision for all this. And there is required for the constitution of such an institution:

1. A sufficient number of men qualified to teach all this; and to carry on original thought and investigation in all this: First of all, we must have the skillful laborers.

2. Books, apparatus, specimens, and models sufficient to furnish all needed information, all needed facilities for scientific and learned investigation, and all needed illustrations. And the men who are to do the work, can alone determine what and how much are needed.

3. Are buildings required? Buildings of course are required. But in our country we have ever begun at the wrong end. We have erected vast dormitories for the night's sleep, instead of creating libraries and laboratories for the day's work. We have erected ornamental buildings, and expending our means and enthusiasm, there, we have failed in the men, the books, the appara-

tus, the specimens, the models. We have had gorgeous shells that seemed like mother of pearl, but there were no pearls within. It were better, like Abelard, to lead our students into the desert, if we could there give them truth and arouse thought.

The Girard College looks like the abode of Apollo and the Muses; but it is only the hospital of some three hundred boys who are instructed in elementary learning, in part if not for the most part, by young women.

All we have to say about buildings, is that we should have only what is necessary, and of a plain, neat, appropriate, and substantial kind.

The instructors or teachers in this circle of human knowledge we divide into Faculties. 1. The Faculty of Philosophy and Science. 2. The Faculty of Literature and the Arts. In the German Universities, these are both embraced under one Faculty—the Faculty of Philosophy. We have here, all branches of knowledge taught, without applying them to any professions, and without those modifications which they receive in this application. Next, we have the Faculty of Theology, or philosophy and science applied to religion and morals—to the great questions of human duty: the Faculty of Law, or philosophy and science applied to jurisprudence and government: and the Faculty of Medicine, or philosophy and science applied to the investigation and cure of diseases. Then in addition to these, there is required a school for the Fine Arts; a school for Agriculturists, Mechanics, Manufacturers, and indeed for every branch of human industry—a school for the Industrial Arts; and a school of Pedagogy, for teaching the philosophy and art of teaching. . . .

A University thus, in its nature and provisions, the highest possible school of learning is, evidently, a school where study may be pursued indefinitely. It may be pursued in reference to particular branches and for a limited time, or it may be pursued for a life time. It may be pursued for a Bachelor's or a Master's degree in one or more faculties, or it may be pursued in particular reference to the Fine or to the Industrial Arts. Whatever a student may need or desire is here to be found. Such is the comprehensive idea of a University.

But the question now arises, at what age, or with what preparation should a student enter a University?

In the first place, there will be a common judgment that a University ought not to embrace the rudiments of knowledge. These can be gained more easily and less expensively in primary schools scattered over the land, and can be united with that domestic influence which is so important to the early education itself. Besides, there are very many who will never look beyond this rudimentary training. And of what avail could the learned professors and preparations of a University be to juvenile students?

But after this primary education is completed, may not the pupil then enter the University? Before we could well answer this, we should have to determine the limits of the primary course. How many studies shall it embrace? Through how many years shall it extend? But the common judgment of mankind seems to have settled this point also. A primary education for the many should embrace whatever is necessary for all men in the general transactions and offices of life; while those who aim at University discipline should make an especial preparation for it. Thus arises the intermediate school. Hence, in all countries where there are primary schools and Universities, there are intermediate schools also.

But now a point remains to be decided between the intermediate school and the University which really comprises our first question: where shall the intermediate or preparatory school close its course; and where shall the University begin?

Now if we look through the leading colleges of our land we shall find that they require about the same amount of preparation for admission; in other words, that they have prescribed about the same limits to the preparatory course. Then again, they have all adopted about the same curriculum of studies, to be pursued during the collegiate years; and they have all adopted four years as the collegiate term, distributing the students into four classes corresponding to these years, naming them Freshman, Sophomore, Junior and Senior. And yet it must be acknowledged that all this does not amount to a University, as we have above described it. Does any College, or University, so called, in our country countain the professors delivering lectures on all branches of human knowledge, and the requisite libraries, and material of learning in general? Is there one of them where a student can study what he pleases, to any extent he pleases, and find every help ready to his hand?

And whence comes this confessedly limited and imperfect course of four years, beginning at a certain point and ending at a certain point; and these four classes with their peculiar titles; and the Baccalaureate degree which winds up the whole; and then the Master's degree, in course, after three years, without requiring any residence, any study, or any examination? We find it all existing among us: but where does it come from? Let me tell you, we have borrowed it from the English Universities: we have borrowed it without enquiring into its fitness: we have simply obeyed an established authority.

If the English Universities were perfect institutions, if they were really Universities, we could not object to their authority. But Sir William Hamilton, the distinguished professor of Logic in the University of Edinburgh, has shewn conclusively in his able articles in the Edinburgh Review, and recently published with his philosophical essays in a separate volume, that the English Universities have deteriorated by departing from their original foundation. . . .

Some peculiarities however, characterise the American colleges. They have professors as well as tutors, and they confer degrees, so that they possess some of the features of a University. They have been, in our days, compelled to advance still further towards this position. This has resulted from the great advancement of the sciences. The four year course was based upon the state of the sciences in former centuries. In modern times it is found wholly inadequate.—We have, indeed, endeavored to keep pace with advancing science by pressing more into the four years; but we have thus, only rendered scholarship more superficial. At length dissatisfied with this we have begun to institute additional courses. Our two oldest colleges have set us the example. Harvard College has established the "Lawrence Scientific School," and attached to it the degree of Bachelor in Science. Yale College has established a "Department of Philosophy and the Arts," intended for graduates of this and other colleges, and "for such other young men as are desirous of pursuing special branches of study," making the proviso, however, that "all students in philology and mathematical science shall be thoroughly grounded in those studies," in order to be admitted. The University of Virginia, and Brown University have thrown aside the four classes with their titles, and establishing courses in the different branches of learning usually pursued at College, admit students at their option, requiring, however the usual attainments for a degree. Other colleges are also endeavoring to modifiy and enlarge their courses.

In all this there is more or less improvement attempted, and a commendable struggle to advance. But in all this there is not yet University amplitude, ripeness and freedom.

It is demonstrable that a system of public education can not only never be complete, but that it can never work with unjarring, noiseless wheels, in the due co-ordination of its parts, without a fully developed University at the lead of the movement. This alone can set the standard of education and define the boundaries of the primary and the intermediate schools; this alone can afford the requisite stimulus to educational efforts, by showing every student the place where all his wants and aspirations can be met; as a beating heart sending its currents of life through the whole, and maintaining the perfection of the organism by visiting the minutest parts.

The manner in which a University determines the limits of other institutions is seen at once when we consider its relation to education historically as well as philosophically considered. "Education, in general, is of two kinds, and of two kinds only: an education imposed by tutors and governors: and an education self-imposed. The first relates to that period of our being embracing childhood and youth, when the faculties are yet immature, and knowledge is in its elementary stages.—The second relates to that period commencing with early manhood, when the faculties are comparatively ripened, when elementary knowledge has been attained, and actual experience has taken the place of imagination and conjecture.

"The first period requires of necessity authoritative direction, and plastic superintendence. The second period is competent, unless the first has been neglected and suffered to run to waste, to form plans, make decisions, exercise choice, and to apply itself, as from itself, to self-culture, the formation of character, and the duties of life.

"All men do, in some sort, attain to both kinds of education: for all men are disciplined in some degree, well or ill, by a controlling power in early life; and all men have some sense of independence and new responsibilities, when they reach the age of manhood. Education, of both kinds, is a law of our being more or less perfectly developed.

"The idea of Educational Institutions, embraces the reduction of educational means and influences to method and system.

"For the first period, various institutions have sprung up, from the most elementary schools to the gymnasia or colleges. For the second period, there is only one institution—the University.

"According to the present condition of our educational system, the higher, self-determined, and manly course of study belonging to this period, is wanting, or appears only as an imperfect appendage to the college under the form of certain voluntary studies, and a limited range of lectures on the loftier sciences, conducted under manifest embarrassments arising from the want of a suitable preparation on the part of the student, and the inadequate amount of time covered by the collegiate course"; or, where in a few instances carried beyond the point of graduation, still wanting in the ample preparations and stimulus of a University. "Hence, where the higher culture is gained, it is gained, rather by studies pursued by the individual amid the duties and cares of life, after the institutions of learning have been departed from, than by means of the institutions themselves. The culture which men, who are determined to make the most of life, attain to amid its active pursuits, is invaluable, and will be prized no less by those who have studied at the University than by those who have not. But who does not see the value, nay, the necessity of an Institution which opens its doors to us just when we escape from governors and tutors, and provides us with all the means, and affords us the example and fellowship of manly self-discipline? It is here alone that we can properly pursue the study of philosophy, which implies more than mere acquisition, and is the self-conscious growth of thought. It is here that we can become disciplined to independent scientific investigation, or lay broad and deep the foundations of professional and political life. It is here, also, that teachers and professors can be prepared for the scientific and classical departments, of our educational institutions in general.

"The University thus stands just where the first period of education closes, and where the other begins. The second period, indeed, never closes. But, as education during the first period, requires, for its orderly developement, institutions of learning; so, education, during the second, requires for its proper determination and successful prosecution, the formation of habits of independent thought and study, an acquaintance with method, and a general survey of the field of knowledge, such as can be gained only in an institution especially founded and furnished for these high ends. The University receives the *alumnus* of the *Alma Mater,* and ripens him into the man prepared for the offices of the Church and the State, and for the service of Science and Letters." *

The intermediate school, by whatever name we call it, embraces the period of a student's apprenticeship, wherein he learns how to study and how to use his books,

* *University Education,* pp. 82–85.

which are his tools. But in the University he begins his manhood, and uses his tools as one who has gained his trade.

The Primary School, the Intermediate School, and the University, now stand before us clearly defined; and these three constitute the educational system founded alike upon philosophy and experience. The Primary has connected with it, as its necessary adjunct, the Normal School. The Intermediate has connected with it, special schools for the arts of industry, where the University is not contemplated. And the University crowns the whole. . . .

There are three grades of schools existing in other parts of the Union. But mark the difference between the Prussian model which we have adopted, and the English which has hitherto been generally adopted in our country. In the first place, the English model contains no common School System. Happily, we have all departed from it, in this respect. Secondly, the English intermediate school and the college are institutions precisely of the same nature. The Schools of Harrow, Rugby, Eton and Winchester, are schools of the same general course of instruction and discipline with the Colleges at Oxford and Cambridge. The latter carry on, in a similar way, what was begun in the former, and confer a degree.

They cover only the first period of Education—that under tutors and governors. The second period—that of manly self-discipline with the aid of the lectures of eminent University professors is not reached in the English system. Oxford and Cambridge contain no schools of Theology, Law, Medicine, and Philosophy.

Now following this system, what are our Academies but incipient Colleges and what are our Colleges but more mature Academies with the power of conferring degrees? And do not young men, often, remain in the Academy until the Sophomore, Junior, and even Senior year? We, too, in our institutions have covered only the first period of education, and left the second period, or, the University proper undeveloped.

There is another respect, too, in which we have followed the English; We have laid out immense sums of money in providing dormitories for Students. Dr. Wayland estimates that of a million and a half invested in New England Colleges, twelve hundred thousand dollars have been expended in brick and mortar. In creating Colleges, we have uniformly begun with two things—the erection of dormitories, and a commencement Exhibition: As if sleeping in cloisters, reciting poems and orations in public, and the conferring of degrees, were essential to the Educational System. Public speaking has its advantages, and to confer degrees, where they are merited, may not be amiss; but why not let young men provide their own board and lodging? Our Colleges are not located in the wilderness, but in pleasant towns where accommodations are abundant.

Now, all this is opposed to the Prussian model. In Prussia, the great aim is to provide libraries, museums, laboratories, observatories, and philosophical apparatus, and a sufficient number of eminent professors. In Prussia, they take care of the great things, and let the small things take care of themselves.

Michigan has the credit of proclaiming the Prussian model. She has wisely adopted the most perfect standard as her standard. Let us see how far she has, already, conformed to it. . . .

In the Literary and Scientific department of the University of Michigan, we find ourselves, at the present moment, in just this condition: We are a University Faculty giving instruction in a College or Gymnasium.

Now, our first object will be to perfect this Gymnasium. To this end, we propose to establish a Scientific course parallel to the classical course. In this scientific course a more extended study of the Mathematics will be substituted for the Greek and Latin. There will be comprised in it, besides other branches, Civil Engineering, Astronomy with the use of an Observatory, and the application of Chemistry and other Sciences to Agriculture and the industrial arts, generally. The entire course will run through four years, in which the Students will be distributed into four classes similarly to the classical course: and in both courses, instead of the old names of *Freshman, Sophomore, Junior,* and *Senior* borrowed from the English colleges, we will take the designations employed in the institutions of the Continent of Europe, of *First, Second, Third,* and *Fourth.*

Students who pursue the full Scientific course, and pass the regular Examinations, we shall graduate as *Bachelors of Science*—borrowing a title here from the French Colleges, as the Lawrence Scientific School of Harvard, and the University of Rochester have done before us—in distinction from the *Bachelors of Arts* in the Classical course.

But, in addition to this, we shall allow Students to select special courses, and give them, at their departure, certificates of their proficiency. The school of civil Engineering, and the school of Agriculture and Mechanics will belong to these special courses.

We shall thus make our College or Gymnasium an Institution where the youth of our State can freely enter to prepare themselves for professional study, for the higher pursuits of Science and Literature, or for the pursuits of business life.

By establishing the scientific course in distinction from the classical, we do not intend to do any discredit to classical learning, or to imply ought in opposition to those who advocate its surpassing value and importance to general and finished Scholarship. . . .

Nor by a distinct scientific course do we mean to lend authority to a vague opposition of a practical to a scholastic education. Human life embraces a great many particulars, and everything which goes to make it up must necessarily belong to it. Now, thinking belongs to it as well as talking; sleeping and dreaming, as well as waking and walking; the fragrance of flowers, the song of the birds, and the sight of the heavens, as well as eating beef and drinking ale; poetry and philosophy and eloquence, as well as ploughing, sowing and reaping; the building of temples, as well as the building of log cabins; the making of statues, pictures and all beautiful things, as well as the making of chairs and tables, spades and hoes and all useful things; there is going to church, as well as going to mill; there are holidays, as well as every-days.

And this human life shews a great many kinds of people—of different colors, ages, sizes, and conditions: and all these kinds of people are about their different things. Now it is the order of creation and providence that this variety should exist. We must take the world just as full as it is. If every one were permitted, according to his fancy or prejudice, to destroy around him to make room for himself alone—what would be left of human life? The distinction between a scholastic and practical education is like all this. Both kinds of education are good and answer somebody's purpose. In truth, a scholastic education is altogether practical to him who desires and wants it. And a practical education becomes quite scholastic to him who does not desire and want it. A farmer may find Chemistry very closely connected with his calling, but what can he do with Latin and Greek and the higher mathematics? But he who is about to make a dictionary or write a history may find Latin and Greek very practical knowledge; and he who is seeking after another planet in the heavens, will tell you that the calculus is the most practical thing he can find. And do not dictionaries, histories, and astronomy belong to human life, too?

The true principle of life for every individual, is, not to quarrel with life in the rest of the world. If thy business is to cut down trees, then go thy way and cut down trees: thou art feeding cheerful household fires, and laying open future harvest fields. If thy business is to sail in a balloon, then go thy way and sail in a balloon; thou art making a needful holiday for the laboring multitude, and trying thy barometer in the heavens. The one has the wide forest for his place, and the other the wider space above. The one may look up, and the other look down, and be pleasant objects to each other. Be ever charitable to each other ye brothers of the human kind! The sky and the earth are still wider apart, and yet they may not be the one without the other.

There is one thing, at least, which the wood-cutter, and

the æronaut have in common; and which the one cannot spare more than the other, although in some sort,
the one is under it, and the other above it; and that is
the air on which they both live. The one would be altogether too low down, and the other altogether too high
up, if they were to get beyond the boundaries of it.

And so likewise heaven and earth, and all worlds have
one thing in common and that is the pure element of
light; and every particle of matter yields to the gravi-
tating power.

Now, there are the lower schools for the education of
human souls: why are they called the lower, but, that
there are others which are higher than they? and if there
are the higher, there must also be the highest. But since
we must have the lowest for earliest years of life, and the
higher for the more developed years of youth, who shall
forbid us the highest for the discipline of manhood? And,
then, as there are different years and conditions to be
educated, and different callings to be fitted for, so there
are a vast variety of knowledges to be gained. There is a
knowledge of the stars of heaven, as well as of the stones of
the earth; a knowledge of men, as well as of beasts, birds,
fishes and insects; a knowledge of organised matter in
plants and animals, as well as of crude matter in the
crust of the earth; a knowledge of languages and music,
as well as of winds and tides; a knowledge of pure science, as well as of mixed science; a knowledge of invisible
forces, as well as of visible motions; a knowledge of the
past as well as of the present; a knowledge of mind, as
well as of matter; a knowledge of law and duty, as well
as of disease and medicine; a knowledge of the divine, as
well as of the human. What shall we do with all these
knowledges? Destroy some of them, or set them aside?
Nay, they are all in God's universe, and cannot be
quenched any more than the stars in heaven; and the
mind of man is made for them all, and as if by a divine
inspiration, will be busy with them all; and all that is
good and beautiful in the world flows out from them.

There are a few minds which have a sort of universal
knowledge: there are others which to a general and im-

perfect comprehension of science, add the ripe knowledge of a few things, or it may be of only one. Some have grasped a great deal of knowledge; others very little. But all these knowledges are scattered somewhere through human minds, exerting their influence for the common good; like the wide streaming light of heaven, which crowning the high mountains with glory, visits also the humblest flowers in the valleys below.

We have described a University as a place where all these knowledges are to be found—a shop of the nine Muses, where they sell their wares to the children of men. Is not that land destitute in which such a place can nowhere be lighted upon? Without such a place, we must want many branches of knowledge, or seek them in other lands. Instead of making our own scholars, and our own books, we must import them, or be without scholars and books.

Suppose all the Universities of Germany were destroyed, where then should we look for their great men whom the world honors, whom we honor—their Schleiermacher, their Neander, their Grimm, their Ritter, their Ehrenberg, their Savigny, their Humboldt? And would not their whole glorious system of education fade away? What would England be without her Universities? And what would America be without her Colleges? The poets, the philosophers, the historians, the wits of England and America where would they be?

Blot out the University of Michigan, young as it is, and would it not seem as if the ancient forests were again overshadowing the land?

This young University, shall we not carry it forward to perfection? Is not the ambition worthy of a free and independent people which would make it one of the great Universities of the world, where all knowledges are to be found, where great and good men are to be reared up, and whence shall go forth the light and law of universal education?

Wilbur F. Storey's
Editorial Assault on Tappan*
(1853)

Tappan's noble aspirations for the University of Michigan were increasingly thwarted as public criticism of his purposes, methods, and personal idiosyncrasies grew in the state. His most determined antagonist was Wilbur F. Storey (1819–1884), a Vermont-born editor who combined the arrogant self-assurance of Isaac Hill with techniques characteristic of a new era in metropolitan journalism. Buying an interest in the Detroit Free Press *in 1853, Storey launched on a career filled with vitriolic personal vendettas, which marked him as a western James Gordon Bennett. A pro-slavery Democrat, his bitter attacks on the Lincoln administration in the* Chicago Times *led to that paper's suspension by military order during the Civil War. Tappan was Storey's first distinguished victim; the occasion for this assault was a report to the Board of Regents, published after the president's return from a trip to Europe in 1853. His themes echoed popular prejudices, and his style was designed to ridicule Tappan's grand manner and affectations.*

THE STATE UNIVERSITY

President TAPPAN's idea of a University is grand—imposing! The German University at Berlin is his model,

---

* *Detroit Free Press,* December 28, 1853; related editorials appeared December 25 and 31. On Storey, see *Dictionary of American Biography,* Vol. XVIII, pp. 97–98.

and he would bring the Wolverine institution up to the Berlin standard with all possible haste. He has a similar idea of cities and towns, though he don't say so in this report. He thinks no city should be without its heaven-pointing monuments and great public works. He conceives that it is a mistake of the Americans that they build warehouses and neglect monuments. He wants to know what will be thought of our country, by future generations, when our structure shall have crumbled, if there shall be no silent, gloomy monuments found, overlooking the general wreck of matter? With a far-stretching vision, he sees America reduced to Egyptian decay, and he is of opinion that we ought to write the history of our rise and progress upon tall monuments for the especial edification of generations that will be yet unborn half a dozen centuries hence! * Something akin to this is his notion of institutions of learning.

One thing is certain, that whether we consider the resources of the State of Michigan and its rapidly advancing greatness, or, its position in reference to surrounding States, we shall neither be true to our own trust, nor shall we pursue a wise policy, if we make our calculations upon a diminuitive scale. Divine Providence has afforded us a great opportunity, and given us indications *which seem almost like a positive command*. To embrace the opportunity, to obey the indications, is the true way of success.

This looks very well on paper to one who has little sense of the ludicrous and the bombastic.—With proper management and steady perseverance—such perseverance as has, after the lapse of a century and a half, made Yale what it is—the University of Michigan can be made one of the first institutions of learning in the country. There is such a thing, especially in educational matters, as going too fast as well as too slow; and often the one is more fatal than the other. A wise statesman makes haste slowly. . . .

* Storey here ridicules one of the themes of Tappan's essay on his experiences in Europe: *A Step from the New World to the Old, and Back Again; with Thoughts on the Good and Evil in Both,* 2 vols. (New York: D. Appleton and Company, 1852).—T.R.C.

At this stage of the report President TAPPAN starts for Berlin:

In speaking of the condition of our University and of what is required for its proper and full development, you will naturally enquire what light I have gained on the subject of education from my visit abroad. This visit, as you are aware, was arranged before I had been called to take charge of the University. It was a fortunate concurrence by which a visit to Europe necessary to be undertaken by some one in respect to the Observatory, and important in respect to the purchase of books and the general interests of our educational system, was accomplished without imposing any expense upon the University.* Besides revisiting England, France, Switzerland, and the Rhine country, I have travelled through Italy, and spent some time in the northern part of Germany, more than two weeks of which was devoted entirely to the examination of the Prussian system of education in the city of Berlin.

We do not understand what President TAPPAN means when he says "besides *re*-visiting England," &c., unless he desires to tell us that this was not the first time he had been to Europe.

A practical man, situated as President TAPPAN was, may unquestionably learn much by an examination of the "Prussian system" which he can make available in the administration of a collegiate institution in this country; but the belief that we want *the* "Prussian system" is preposterous. We want just so much of it as can be profitably adapted to our altered system of government, of trade, of commerce, and so forth. To make this adaptation, requires great judgment and caution—a thorough understanding of the genius of our institutions, and of the educational necessities of our people. Our schools, and academies, and universities need to be *American* rather than Prussian—that is, instead of treading in a mere beaten track, we want institutions that shall fit men for all the practical duties of American life—that shall strike out in the wilderness of progress—availing themselves of the new philosophy, and rejecting all of the old that is not instinct with life and spirit.

* President Tappan was under pay both from the University and from a private source during his "visit abroad."

Our faith is not the strongest, after reading this report, that President TAPPAN is quite likely to accommodate himself to things as they exist here, and proceed cautiously in gradually enlarging the capacity and power of our University. With the University of Berlin for his idol, he seems in danger of forgetting that Michigan is not Prussia, and Ann Arbor not Berlin. He anticipates a scale of operations that the present resources of the University will not justify, and calculates upon direct aid regularly hereafter from the State Treasury that the sequel will not realize. With many just and enlightened views he combines projects that are at once impracticable and visionary.

The first interrogatory, viz: "what is yet to be done"? is answered, then, mainly by a recommendation to adopt the Prussian system, including the high University and Gymnasium, and "special schools for the useful and fine arts"—a system of such huge proportions that it must indeed become a government institution—a central power greater than the State itself, and involving an annual outlay from the treasury larger than the gross expenditures for the support of the State government!

The answer to the other interrogatory, "how shall we do it?" is already anticipated. But President TAPPAN does not mince the matter; he declares:

The sale of our lands from year to year will continue to add to our income, until we have realised all which this source of income can afford us. *Beyond this we must look mainly to the State.*

To what extent the people of Michigan will feel inclined to maintain a grand Prussian University at Ann Arbor by direct appropriations from the public treasury is a pretty grave question. We have no hesitation in saying, in the outset, as one of the people, that we are hostile to any such use of money that is drawn from the pockets of the whole people. If the permanent endowment of the University is not sufficient to support it, it must tax the recipients of its benefits to make up the deficiency. . . .

11. Jonathan Baldwin Turner:

*Plan for an Industrial University, for the State of Illinois** (1851)

*A Yale graduate who taught at Illinois College, Jackson-
ville, from 1833 to 1847, Jonathan Baldwin Turner
(1805–1899) was an important figure in the educational
history of his adopted state. During the 1850's he was the
principal lobbyist for the Illinois Industrial League,
which was dedicated to the promotion of advanced education for mechanics and farmers. The following document, prepared for a convention in Granville, Illinois,
in 1851, contains a full statement of Turner's program.
Written in homespun style, an assault on the learned
professions that recalls William Manning's prejudices is
coupled with proposals for institutional development
that forecast the vocational emphasis of many twentieth-
century universities.*

* "Plan for an Industrial University, for the State of Illinois,"
in J. B. Turner, *Industrial Universities for the People. Published in
Compliance with Resolutions of the Chicago and Springfield Conventions, and under the Industrial League of Illinois*, 2nd ed. (Chicago: Robert Fergus, Printer, 1854), pp. 18–33. Turner's contribution
to the Morrill Act of 1862 is overemphasized in Edmund J. James,
*The Origin of the Land Grant Act of 1862 (The So-Called Morrill
Act) and Some Account of Its Author, Jonathan B. Turner*, University of Illinois, The University Studies, Vol. IV, No. 1 (Urbana-
Champaign, Illinois: University Press, 1910). Earle D. Ross, *Democracy's College: The Land-Grant Movement in the Formative Stage*
(Ames, Iowa: Iowa State College Press, 1942), provides a more bal-
anced treatment of the origins of the Morrill Act and an account of
the early development of those institutions which received its benefits. A family memoir of Turner, containing speeches, letters, and
essays, first published in 1911, has recently been reissued: Mary
Turner Carriel, *The Life of Jonathan Baldwin Turner* (Urbana,
Illinois: University of Illinois Press, 1961).

All civilized society is, necessarily, divided into two distinct cooperative, not antagonistic, classes:—a small class, whose proper business it is to teach the true principles of religion, law, medicine, science, art, and literature; and a much larger class, who are engaged in some form of labor in agriculture, commerce, and the arts. For the sake of convenience, we will designate the former the PROFESSIONAL, and the latter the INDUSTRIAL class; not implying that each may not be equally industrious: the one in their intellectual, the other in their industrial pursuits. Probably, in no case would society ever need more than five men out of one hundred in the professional class, leaving ninety-five in every hundred in the industrial; and so long as so many of our ordinary teachers and public men are taken from the industrial class, as there are at present, and probably will be for generations to come, we do not really need over one professional man for every hundred, leaving ninety-nine in the industrial class.

The vast difference, in the practical means, of an APPROPRIATE LIBERAL EDUCATION, suited to their wants and their destiny, which these two classes enjoy, and ever have enjoyed the world over, must have arrested the attention of every thinking man. True, the same general abstract science exists in the world for both classes alike, but the means of bringing this abstract truth into effectual contact with the daily business and pursuits of the one class does exist, while in the other case it does not exist, and never can, till it is new created.

The one class have schools, seminaries, colleges, universities, apparatus, professors, and multitudinous appliances for educating and training them for months and years, for the peculiar profession which is to be the business of their life; and they have already created, each class for its own use, a vast and voluminous literature, that would well nigh sink a whole navy of ships.

But where are the universities, the apparatus, the professors, and the literature, specifically adapted to any one of the industrial classes? Echo answers, where? In other words, society has become, long since, wise enough to know that its TEACHERS need to be educated; but it has not yet become wise enough to know that its WORKERS need education just as much. In these remarks I have not forgotten that our common schools are equally adapted and applied to all classes; but reading, writing, &c., are, properly, no more education than gathering seed is agriculture, or cutting ship-timber navigation. They are the mere rudiments, as they are called, or means, the mere instrument of an after education, and if not so used they are, and can be, of little more use to the possessor than an axe in the garret or a ship rotting upon the stocks.

Nor am I unmindful of the efforts of the monarchs and aristocrats of the old world in founding schools for the "fifteenth cousins" of their order, in hopes of training them into a sort of *genteel farmers,* or rather *overseers* of farmers; nor yet, of the several "back fires" (as the Prairie Farmer significantly designates them) set by some of our older professional institutions, to keep the rising and blazing thought of the industrial masses from burning too furiously. They have hauled a canoe alongside of their huge professional steamships, and invited all the farmers and mechanics of the State to jump on board and sail with them; but the difficulty is, they will not embark. But we thank them even for this pains and courtesy. It shows that their hearts are yearning toward us, notwithstanding the ludicrous awkwardness of their first endeavors to save us.

But an answer to two simple questions will perhaps sufficiently indicate our ideas of the whole subject, though that answer, on the present occasion, must necessarily be confined to a bare outline. The first question, then, is this:

I. WHAT DO THE INDUSTRIAL CLASSES WANT?

II. HOW CAN THAT WANT BE SUPPLIED?

The first question may be answered in few words. They want, and they ought to have, the same facilities for understanding the true philosophy—the science and the art of their several pursuits, (their life-business,) and of efficiently applying existing knowledge thereto and widening its domain, which the professional classes have long enjoyed in their pursuits. Their first labor is, therefore, to supply a vacuum from fountains already full, and bring the living waters of knowledge within their own reach. Their second is, to help fill the fountains with still greater supplies. They desire to depress no institution, no class whatever; they only wish to elevate themselves and their pursuits to a position in society to which all men acknowledge they are justly entitled, and to which they also desire to see them aspire.

II. How then can that want be supplied?

In answering this question, I shall endeavor to present, with all possible frankness and clearness, the outline of impressions and convictions that have been gradually deepening in my own mind, for the past twenty years, and let them pass for whatever the true friends of the cause may think them worth.

And I answer, first, negatively, that this want cannot be supplied by any of the existing institutions for the professional classes, nor by any incidental appendage attached to them as a mere secondary department.

These institutions were designed and adapted to meet the wants of the professional classes, as such—especially the clerical order; and they are no more suited to the real wants of the industrial class than the institution we propose for them, would be suited to the professional class.

Their whole spirit and aim is, or should be, literary and intellectual—not practical and industrial; to make men of books and ready speech—not men of work, and industrial, silent thought.—But, the very best classical scholars are often the very worst practical reasoners; and that they should be made workers is contrary to the nature of things—the fixed laws of God. The whole interest, business, and destiny for life of the two classes, run in opposite lines; and that the same course of study should be equally well adapted to both, is as utterly impossible as that the same pursuits and habits should equally concern and befit both classes.

The industrial classes know and feel this, and therefore they do not, and will not, patronize these institutions, only so far forth as they desire to make professional men for public use. As a general fact, their own multitudes do, and *will forever,* stand aloof from them; and, while they desire to foster and cherish them for their own appropriate uses, they know that they do not, and cannot, fill the sphere of their own urgent industrial wants. They need a similar system of *liberal education* for their own class, and adapted to their own pursuits; to create for them an INDUSTRIAL LITERATURE, adapted to their professional wants, to raise up for them *teachers* and *lecturers,* for subordinate institutes, and to elevate them, their pursuits, and their posterity to that relative position in human society for which God designed them.

The whole history of education, both in Protestant and Catholic countries, shows that we must begin with the higher institutions, or we can never succeed with the lower; for the plain reason, that neither knowledge nor water will run up hill. No people ever had, or ever can have, any system of common schools and lower seminaries worth anything, until they first founded their higher institutions and fountains of knowledge from which they could draw supplies of teachers, &c., for the lower. We would begin, therefore, where all experience and common sense show that we must begin, if we would effect anything worthy of an effort.

In this view of the case, the first thing wanted in this process is a NATIONAL INSTITUTE OF SCIENCE, to operate as the great central luminary of the national mind, from which all minor institutions should derive light and heat, and toward which they should, also, reflect back their own. This primary want is already, I trust, supplied by the Smithsonian Institute, endowed by James Smithson, and incorporated by the U. S. Congress, at Washington, D. C.

To co-operate with this noble Institute, and enable the industrial classes to realize its benefits in practical life, we need a *University for the Industrial Classes* in each of the States, with their consequent subordinate institutes, lyceums, and high schools, in each of the counties and towns.

The objects of these institutes should be to apply existing knowledge directly and efficiently to all practical pursuits and professions in life, and to extend the boundaries of our present knowledge in all possible practical directions.

PLAN FOR THE STATE UNIVERSITY

There should be connected with such an institution, in this State, a sufficient quantity of land of variable soil and aspect, for all its needful annual experiments and processes in the great interests of Agriculture and Horticulture.

Buildings of appropriate size and construction for all its ordinary and special uses; a complete philosophical, chemical, anatomical, and industrial apparatus; a general cabinet, embracing everything that relates to, illustrates or facilitates any one of the industrial arts; especially all sorts of animals, birds, reptiles, insects, trees, shrubs, and plants found in this State and adjacent States.

Instruction should be constantly given in the anatomy and physiology, the nature, instincts, and habits of animals, insects, trees, and plants; their laws of propagation, primogeniture, growth, and decay, disease and health, life and death, on the nature, composition, adaptation, and regeneration of soils; on the nature, strength, durability, preservation, perfection, composition, cost, use, and manufacture of all materials of art and trade; on political, financial, domestic, and manual economy, (or the saving of labor of the hand,) in all industrial processes; on the true principles of national, constitutional, and civil law; and the true theory and art of governing and controlling, or directing the labor of men in the State, the family, shop, and farm; on the laws of vicinage, or the laws of courtesy and comity between neighbors, as such, and on the principles of health and disease in the human subject, so far at least as is needful for household safety; on the laws of trade and commerce, ethical, conventional, and practical; on book-keeping and accounts; and, in short, in all those studies and sciences, of whatever sort, which tend to throw light upon any art or employment, which any student may desire to master, or upon any duty he may be called to perform; or which may tend to secure his moral, civil, social, and industrial perfection, as a man.

No species of knowledge should be excluded, practical or theoretical; unless, indeed, those specimens of "organized ignorance" found in the creeds of party politicians and sectarian ecclesiastics should be mistaken by some for a species of knowledge.

Whether a distinct classical department should be added or not, would depend on expediency. It might be deemed best to leave that department to existing colleges as their more appropriate work, and to form some practical and economical connection with them for that purpose; or it might be best to attach a classical department in due time to the institution itself.

To facilitate the increase and practical application and diffusion of knowledge, the professors should conduct, each in his own department, a continued series of *annual experiments*.

For example, let twenty or more acres of each variety of grain, (each acre accurately measured,) be annually sown, with some practical variation on each acre, as regards the quality and preparation of the soil, the kind and quantity of seed, the time and mode of sowing or planting, the time, and modes, and processes of cultivation and harvesting, and an accurate account kept of all costs, labor, &c., and of the final results. Let analogous experiments be tried on all the varied products of the farm, the fruit yard, the nursery, and the garden; on all modes of crossing, rearing, and fattening domestic animals, under various degrees of warmth and of light, with and without shelter; on green, dry, raw, ground, and cooked food, cold and warm; on the nature, causes, and cure of their various diseases, both of those on the premises and of those brought in from abroad, and advice given, and annual reports made on those and all similar topics. . . .

The APPARATUS required for such a work is obvious. There should be grounds devoted to a botanical and common garden, to orchards and fruit yards, to appropriate lawns and promenades, in which the beautiful art of landscape gardening could be appropriately applied and illustrated, to all varieties of pasture, meadow, and tillage needful for the successful prosecution of the needful annual experiments. And on these grounds should be collected and exhibited a sample of every variety of domestic animal, and of every tree, plant, and vegetable that can minister to the health, wealth, or taste and comfort of the people of the State; their nature, habits, merits, production, improvement, culture, diseases, and accidents thoroughly scrutinized, tested, and made known to the students and to the people of the State.

There should, also, be erected a sufficient number of buildings and out-buildings for all the purposes above indicated, and a REPOSITORY, in which all the ordinary tools and implements of the institution should be kept, and models of all other useful implements and machines from time to time collected, and tested as they are proffered to public use. At first it would be for the interest of inventors and vendors to make such deposits. But should similar institutions be adopted in other States, the general government ought to create in each State a general patent office, attached to the Universities, similar to the existing deposits at Washington, thus rendering this department of mechanical art and skill more accessible to the great mass of the people of the Union.

I should have said, also, that a suitable industrial library should be at once procured, did not all the world know such a thing to be impossible, and that one of the first and most important duties of the professors of such institutions will be to begin to create, at this late hour, a proper practical literature, and series of text books for the industrial classes.

As regards the PROFESSORS, they should, of course, not

only be men of the most eminent practical ability in their several departments, but their connexion with the institution should be rendered so fixed and stable, as to enable them to carry through such designs as they may form, or all the peculiar benefits of the system would be lost.

Instruction, by lectures or otherwise, should be given mostly in the coldest months of the year; leaving the professors to prosecute their investigations, and the students their necessary labor, either at home or on the premises, during the warmer months.

The institution should be open to all classes of students above a fixed age, and for any length of time, whether three months or seven years, and each taught in those particular branches of art which he wishes to pursue, and to any extent, more or less. And all should pay their tuition and board bills, in whole or in part, either in money or necessary work on the premises—regard being had to the ability of each.

Among those who labor, medals and testimonials of merit should be given to those who perform their task with most promptitude, energy, care, and skill; and all who prove indolent or ungovernable, excluded at first from all part in labor, and speedily, if not thoroughly reformed, from the institution itself; and here again let the law of nature instead of the law of rakes and dandies be regarded, and the true impression ever made on the mind of all around, that WORK ALONE IS HONORABLE, and indolence certain disgrace if not ruin.

At some convenient season of the year, the Commencement, or ANNUAL FAIR of the University, should be holden through a succession of days. On this occasion the doors of the institution, with all its treasures of art and resources of knowledge, should be thrown open to all classes, and as many other objects of agricultural or mechanical skill, gathered from the whole State, as possible, and presented by the people for inspection and premium on the best of each kind; judgment being rendered, in all cases, by a committee wholly disconnected with the institution. On this occasion, all the professors, and as many of the pupils as are sufficiently advanced, should be constantly engaged in lecturing and explaining the divers objects and interests of their departments. In short, this occasion should be made the great annual GALA-DAY of the Institution, and of all the industrial classes, and all other classes in the State, for the exhibition of their products and their skill, and for the vigorous and powerful diffusion of practical knowledge in their ranks, and a more intense enthusiasm in its extension and pursuit.

As matters now are, the world has never adopted any efficient means for the application and diffusion of even the practical knowledge which does exist. True, we have fairly got the primer, the spelling book, and the newspaper abroad in the world, and we think that we have done wonders; and so, comparatively, we have. But if this is a wonder, there are still not only wonders, but, to most minds, inconceivable miracles, from new and unknown worlds of light, soon to burst forth upon the industrial mind of the world.

Here, then, is a general, though very incomplete outline of what such an institution should endeavor to become. Let the reader contemplate it as it will appear when generations have perfected it, in all its magnificence and glory; in its means of good to man, to *all men* of *all classes;* in its power to evolve and diffuse practical knowledge and skill, true taste, love of industry, and sound morality—not only through its apparatus, experiments, instructions, and annual lectures and reports, but through its thousands of graduates, in every pursuit in life, teaching and lecturing in all our towns and villages; and then let him seriously ask himself, is not such an object worthy of at least an effort, and worthy of a state which God himself, in the very act of creation, designed to be the first agricultural and commercial State on the face of the globe?

Who should set the world so glorious an example of educating their sons worthily of their heritage, their duty, and their destiny, if not the people of such a State? In our country, we have no aristocracy, with the inalienable wealth of ages and constant leisure and means to perform all manner of useful experiments for their own amusement; but we must create our nobility for this purpose, as we elect our rulers, from our own ranks, to aid and serve, not to domineer over and control us. And this done, we will not only beat England, and beat the world in yachts, and locks, and reapers, but in all else that contributes to the well being and true glory of man.

I maintain that, if every farmer's and mechanic's son in this State could now visit such an institution but for a single day in the year, it would do him more good in arousing and directing the dormant energies of mind, than all the cost incurred, and far more good than many a six months of professed study of things he will never need and never want to know.

As things now are, our best farmers and mechanics, by their own native force of mind, by the slow process of individual experience, come to know, at forty, what they might have been taught in six months at twenty; while a still greater number of the less fortunate or less gifted, stumble on through life, almost as ignorant of every true principle of their art as when they begun. A man of real skill is amazed at the slovenly ignorance and waste he everywhere discovers, on all parts of their premises; and still more to hear them boast of their ignorance of all "book farming," and maintain that "their children can do as well as they have done;" and it certainly would be a great pity if they could not.

The patrons of our University would be found in the former, not in the latter class. The man whose highest conception of earthly bliss is a log hut, in an unenclosed yard, where pigs of two species are allowed equal rights, unless the four-legged tribe chance to get the upper hand, will be found no patron of Industrial Universities. Why should he be? He knows it already.

There is another class of untaught farmers who devote all their capital and hired labor to the culture, on a large scale, of some single product, which always pays well when so produced on a fresh soil, even in the most unskilful hands. Now, such men often increase rapidly in wealth, but it is not by their skill in agriculture, for they have none; their skill consists in the management of capital and labor, and, deprive them of these, and confine them to the varied culture of a small farm, and they would starve in five years, where a true farmer would amass a small fortune. This class are, however, generally the fast friends of education, though many a looker-on will cite them as instances of the uselessness of acquired skill in farming, whereas they should cite them only as a sample of the resistless power of capital even in comparatively unskilful hands.

Such institutions are the only possible remedy for a caste education, legislation, and literature. If any one class provide for their own liberal education, in the State, as they should do, while another class neglect this, it is as inevitable as the law of gravitation, that they should form a ruling caste or class by themselves, and wield their power more or less for their own exclusive interests and the interests of their friends.

If the industrial were the only educated class in the State, the caste power in their hands would be as much stronger than it now is, as their numbers are greater. But now industrial education has been wholly neglected, and the various industrial classes left still ignorant of matters of the greatest moment pertaining to their vital interests, while the professions have been studied till trifles and fooleries have been magnified into matters of immense importance, and tornadoes of windy words and barrels of innocent ink shed over them in vain.

This, too, is the inevitable result of trying to crowd all liberal, practical education into one narrow sphere of human life. It crowds their ranks with men totally unfit by nature for professional service. Many of these, under a more congenial culture, might have become, instead of the starving scavengers of a learned profession, the honored members of an industrial one. Their love of knowledge was indeed amiable and highly commendable; but the necessity which drove them from their natural sphere in life, in order to obtain it, is truly deplorable.

But such a system of general education as we now propose would (in ways too numerous now to mention) tend to increase the respectability, power, numbers, and resources of the true professional class.

Nor are the advantages of the mental and moral discipline of the student to be overlooked; indeed, I should have set them down as most important of all, had I not been distinctly aware that such an opinion is a most deadly heresy; and I tremble at the thought of being arraigned before the tribunal of all the monks and ecclesiastics of the old world, and no small number of their progeny in the new.

It is deemed highly important that all in the professional classes should become writers and talkers; hence they are so incessantly drilled in all the forms of language, dead and living, though it has become quite doubtful whether, even in their case, such a course is most beneficial, except in the single case of the professors of literature and theology, with whom these languages form the foundation of their profes   as, and the indispensable instruments of their future   in life.

No inconsiderable sha   however, of the mental discipline that is attribute   this peculiar course of study, arises from daily int   urse, for years, with minds of the first order in their teachers and comrades, and would be produced under any other course, if the parties remained harmoniously together. On the other hand, a classical teacher who has no original, spontaneous power of thought, and knows nothing but Latin and Greek, however perfectly, is enough to stultify a whole generation of boys, and make them all pedantic fools like himself. The idea of infusing mind, or creating, or even materially increasing it, by the mere daily inculcation of unintelligible words, will, at any rate, never succeed except in the hands of the eminently wise and prudent, who have had long experience in the process; the plain, blunt sense of the unsophisticated will never realize cost in the operation. There are moreover, probably, few men who do not already talk more, in proportion to what they really know, than they ought to. This chronic diarrhœa of exhortation, which the social atmosphere of the age tends to engender, tends far less to public health than many suppose. The history of the Quakers shows that more sound sense, a purer morality, and a more elevated, practical piety can exist, and does exist, entirely without it, than is commonly found with it.

At all events we find, as society becomes less conservative and pedantic, and more truly and practically enlightened, a growing tendency of all other classes, except the literary and clerical, to omit this supposed linguistic discipline, and apply themselves directly to the more immediate duties of their calling; and, aside from some little inconvenience at first in being outside of caste, that they do not succeed quite as well in advancing their own interests in life, and the true interests of society, there is no sufficient proof. . . .

The most natural and effectual mental discipline possible for any man, arises from setting him to earnest and constant thought about the things he daily does, sees, and handles, and all their connected relations and interests. The final object to be attained with the industrial class, is to make them THINKING LABORERS; while of the professional class we should desire to make LABORIOUS THINKERS: the production of goods to feed and adorn the body being the final end of one class of pursuits; and the production of thought, to do the same for the mind, the end of the other. But neither mind nor body can feed on the offals of preceding generations. And this constantly recurring necessity of re-production leaves an equally honorable, though somewhat different, career of labor and duty open to both, and, it is readily admitted, should and must vary their modes of education and preparation accordingly.

It may do for the man of books to plunge at once amid the catacombs of buried nations and languages, to soar away to Greece, or Rome, or Nova-Zembla, Kamtschatka, and the fixed stars, before he knows how to plant his own beans, or harness his own horse, or can tell whether the functions of his own body are performed by a heart, stomach, and lungs, or with a gizzard and gills.

But for the man of work thus to bolt away at once from himself and all his pursuits in after-life, contravenes the plainest principles of nature and common sense. No wonder such educators have ever deemed the liberal culture of the industrial classes an impossibility; for they have never tried nor even conceived of any other way of educating them, except that by which they are rendered totally unfit for their several callings in after-life. How absurd it would seem to set a clergyman to plowing, and studying the depredations of blights, insects, the growing of crops, &c., &c., in order to give him habits of thought and mental discipline for the pulpit; yet this is not half as ridiculous, in reality, as the reverse absurdity of attempting to educate the man of work in unknown tongues, abstract problems and theories, and metaphysical figments and quibbles.

Some, doubtless, will regard the themes of such a course of education as too sensuous and gross to lie at the basis of a pure and elevated mental culture. But the themes themselves cover all possible knowledge, and all modes and phases of science, abstract, mixed, and practical. In short, the field embraces all that God has made, and all that human art has done; and if the created universe of God and the highest art of man are too gross for our refined uses, it is a pity the "morning stars and the sons of God" did not find it out as soon as the blunder was made. But, in my opinion, these topics are of quite as much consequence to the well-being of man and the healthful development of mind, as the concoction of the final nostrum in medicine, or the ultimate figment in theology and law, conjectures about the galaxy or the Greek accent; unless, indeed, the pedantic professional trifles of one man in a thousand are of more consequence than the daily vital interests of all the rest of mankind.

But can such an institution be created and endowed? Doubtless it can be done, and done at once, if the industrial classes so decide. The fund given to this State by the General Government, expressly for this purpose, is amply sufficient, without a dollar from any other source; and it is a mean, if not an illegal, perversion of this fund, to use it for any other purpose. It was given to the people, the whole people, of this State; not for a class, a party, or sect, or conglomeration of sects; not for common schools, or family schools, or classical schools; but for "An University," or Seminary, of a high order, in which should of course be taught all those things which every class of the citizens most desire to learn—their own duty and business for life. This, and this alone, is an University in the true, original sense of the term. And if an institution which teaches all that is needful only for the three professions of law, divinity, and medicine, is, therefore, an University, surely one which teaches all that is needful for all the varied professions of human life is far more deserving of the name and the endowments of an University.

But in whose hands shall the guardianship and oversight of this fund be placed, in order to make it of any real use for such a purpose? I answer, without hesitation and without fear, that this whole interest should, from the first, be placed directly in the hands of the people, and the whole people, without any mediators or advisers, legislative or ecclesiastical, save only their own appointed agents, and their own jurors and courts of justice, to which, of course, all alike must submit. It was given to the people, and is the property of the people, not of legislators, parties or sects, and they ought to have the whole control of it, so far as is possible, consistently with a due security of the funds and needful stability of plans of action and instruction. This control I believe they will be found abundantly able to exercise; and more than this no well-informed man would desire.

The reasons for placing it at once and forever beyond all legislative and ecclesiastical control, are obvious to all. For if, under the former, it may continually exist as the mere tool of the dominant party, and the object of jealous fear and hatred of their opponents, or become the mere foot-ball of all parties, to be kicked hither and thither as the party interests and passion of the hour may dictate. We well know how many millions of money have been worse than thrown away by placing professed seminaries of learning under the influence of party passion, through legislative control. And it is surely a matter of devout gratitude that our legislators have had wisdom enough to see and feel this difficulty, and that they have been led, from various causes, to hold this fund free from all commitment to the present hour, when the people begin to be convinced that they need it, and can safely control it; and no legislator, but an aristocrat or a demagogue, would desire to see it in other hands.

The same difficulty occurs as regards to sects. Let the institution be managed ever so well by any one party or sect, it is still certain their opponents will stand aloof from it, if not oppose and malign it, for that very reason. Hence, all will see at once that the greatest possible care should be taken to free it from, not only the reality, but even from the *suspicion,* of any such influence. . . .

Let the Governor of the State nominate a Board of Trust for the funds of the Institution. Let this Board consist of five of the most able and discreet men in the State, and let at least four of them be taken from each of the extreme corners of the State, so remote from all proximity to the possible location of the Institution, both in person and in property, as to be free from all suspicion of partiality. Let the Senate confirm such nomination. Let this Board be sworn to locate the Institution from a regard to the interests and convenience of the people of the whole State; and when they have so done, let them be empowered to elect twelve new members of their own body, with perpetual power of filling their own vacancies, each choice requiring a vote of two-thirds of the whole body, and upon any failure to elect at the appointed annual meeting, the Governor of the State to fill the vacancy for one year, if requested by any member of the Board so to do. Let any member of the Board who shall be absent from any part of its annual meetings, thereby forfeit his seat, unless detained by sickness, certified at the time, and the Board on that occasion fill the vacancy, either by his re-election or by the choice of some other man. Let the funds then, by the same act, pass into the hands of the trustees so organized, as a perpetual trust, they giving proper bonds for the same, to be used for the endowment and erection of an Industrial University for the State of Illinois.

This Board, so constituted, would be, and ought to be, responsible to no legislature, sect, or party, but directly to the people themselves—to each and every citizen, in the courts of law and justice; so that, should any trustee of the institution neglect, abuse, or pervert his trust to any selfish, local, political, or sectarian end, or show himself incompetent for its exercise, every other member of the Board, and every citizen at large, should have the right of impeaching him before the court, and, if guilty, the court should discharge him, and order his place to be filled by a more suitable man. Due care should be taken, of course, to guard against malicious prosecutions.

Doubtless, objections can be urged against this plan, and all others that can be proposed. Most of them may be at once anticipated, but there is not space enough to notice them here. Some, for example, cherish an ardent and praiseworthy desire for the perfection of our common schools, and desire still longer to use that fund for that purpose. But no one imagines that it can long be kept for that use; and if it could, I think it plain that the lower schools of all sorts would be far more benefited by it here than in any other place it could be put.

Others may feel a little alarm, when, for the first time in the history of the world, they see the millions throwing themseves aloof from all political and ecclesiastical control, and attempting to devise a system of liberal education for themselves; but on mature reflection we trust they will approve the plan; or, if they are too old to change, their children will.

I shall enter upon no special pleas in favor of this plan of disposing of our State fund. I am so situated in life that it cannot possibly do me any personal good, save only in the just pride of seeing the interests of my brethren of the industrial class cared for and promoted, as in such an age and such a State they ought to be. If they want the benefit of such an institution they can have it. If they do not want it, I have not another word to say. In their own will, alone, lies their own destiny, and that of their children.

Respectfully submitted,

J. B. TURNER.

12. The Morrill Act*

(1862)

When the Illinois legislature endorsed Turner's scheme for industrial universities in 1853, it requested that they be endowed from the public domain. The cause had eastern champions also; its leader in Congress was Justin Smith Morrill (1810–1898), Representative from Vermont. Morrill's first bill authorizing federal aid was vetoed by President Buchanan in 1859, but a second was signed by Abraham Lincoln on July 2, 1862. Public lands were offered to each state in proportion to its representation in Congress; hence, eastern colleges might benefit from the resources of western states, and the objective of free farms for pioneers, embodied in the Homestead Act of the same year, was compromised. But the principle of federal support for higher education had been established, not in the central university George Washington had advocated, but in decentralized colleges adapted to the needs of all classes. The Civil War crisis led to the requirement that all land-grant colleges provide military training, but otherwise their nature was largely unspecified. The strongest institutions to profit from the act, such as Cornell and Wisconsin, used Morrill endowment to support technical training within a comprehensive university and also sought distinction in the liberal arts.

* Text from G. Brown Goode, "The Origin of the National Scientific and Educational Institutions of the United States," in American Historical Association, *Annual Report for the Year 1889* (Washington, D.C.: Government Printing Office, 1890), pp. 146–148. For further background, see Paul W. Gates, "Western Opposition to the Agricultural College Act," *Indiana Magazine of History*, XXXVII, March 1941 [*sic*, i.e., June 1941], 103–136. On Morrill, see William Belmont Parker, *The Life and Public Services of Justin Smith Morrill* (Boston: Houghton Mifflin Company, 1924), especially Chapter 11.

AN ACT DONATING PUBLIC LANDS TO THE SEVERAL STATES AND TERRITORIES WHICH MAY PROVIDE COLLEGES FOR THE BENEFIT OF AGRICULTURE AND MECHANIC ARTS

Be it enacted by the Senate and House of Representatives of the United States of America in Congress assembled, That there be granted to the several States, for the purposes hereinafter mentioned, an amount of public land, to be apportioned to each State a quantity equal to thirty thousand acres for each senator and representative in Congress to which the States are respectively entitled by the apportionment under the census of eighteen hundred and sixty: *Provided,* That no mineral lands shall be selected or purchased under the provisions of this act.

SEC. 2. *And be it further enacted.* That the land aforesaid, after being surveyed, shall be apportioned to the several States in sections or subdivisions of sections, not less than one quarter of a section; and whenever there are public lands in a State subject to sale at private entry at one dollar and twenty-five cents per acre, the quantity to which said State shall be entitled shall be selected from such lands within the limits of such State, and the Secretary of the Interior is hereby directed to issue to each of the States in which there is not the quantity of public lands subject to sale at private entry at one dollar and twenty-five cents per acre, to which said State may be entitled under the provisions of this act, land scrip to the amount in acres for the deficiency of its distributive share; said scrip to be sold by said States and the proceeds thereof applied to the uses and purposes prescribed in this act, and for no other use or purpose whatsoever: *Provided,* That in no case shall any State to which land scrip may thus be issued be allowed to locate the same within the limits of any other State, or of any Territory of the United States, but their assignees may thus locate said land scrip upon any of the unappropriated lands of the United States subject to sale at private entry at one dollar and twenty-five cents, or less, per acre: *And provided further,* That not more than one million acres shall be located by such assignees in any one of the States: *And provided further,* That no such location shall be made before one year from the passage of this act.

Sec. 3. *And be it further enacted,* That all the expenses of management, superintendence, and taxes from date of selection of said lands, previous to their sales, and all expenses incurred in the management and disbursement of the moneys which may be received therefrom, shall be paid by the States to which they may belong, out of the treasury of said States, so that the entire proceeds of the sale of said lands shall be applied without any diminution whatever to the purposes hereinafter mentioned.

Sec. 4. *And be it further enacted,* That all moneys derived from the sale of the lands aforesaid by the State to which the lands are apportioned, and from the sales of land scrip hereinbefore provided for, shall be invested in stocks of the United States, or of the States, or some other safe stocks, yielding not less than five per centum upon the par value of said stocks; and that the moneys so invested shall constitute a perpetual fund, the capital of which shall remain forever undiminished, (except so far as may be provided in section fifth of this act,) and the interest of which shall be inviolably appropriated, by each State which may take and claim the benefit of this act, to the endowment, support, and maintenance of at least one college where the leading object shall be, without excluding other scientific and classical studies, and including military tactics, to teach such branches of learning as are related to agriculture and the mechanic arts, in such manner as the legislatures of the States may respectively prescribe, in order to promote the liberal and practical education of the industrial classes in the several pursuits and professions in life.

Sec. 5. *And be it further enacted,* That the grant of land and land scrip hereby authorized shall be made on the following conditions, to which, as well as to the provisions hereinbefore contained, the previous assent of the several States shall be signified by legislative acts:

First.   If any portion of the fund invested, as provided by the foregoing section, or any portion of the interest thereon, shall, by any action or contingency be diminished or lost, it shall be replaced by the State to which it belongs, so that the capital of the fund shall remain forever undiminished; and the annual interest shall be regularly applied without diminution to the purposes mentioned in the fourth section of this act, except that a sum, not exceeding ten per centum upon the amount received by any State under the provisions of this act, may be expended for the purchase of lands for sites or experimental farms, whenever authorized by the respective legislatures of said States.

Second.   No portion of said fund, nor the interest thereon, shall be applied, directly or indirectly, under any pretense whatever, to the purchase, erection, preservation, or repair of any building or buildings.

Third.   Any State which may take and claim the benefit of the provisions of this act shall provide, within five years, at least not less than one college, as described in the fourth section of this act, or the grant to such State shall cease; and said State shall be bound to pay the United States the amount received of any lands previously sold, and that the title to purchasers under the State shall be valid.

Fourth. An annual report shall be made regarding the progress of each college, recording any improvements and experiments made, with their costs and results, and such other matters, including State industrial and economical statistics, as may be supposed useful; one copy of which shall be transmitted by mail free, by each, to all the other colleges which may be endowed under the provisions of this act, and also one copy to Secretary of the Interior.

Fifth.   When lands shall be selected from those which have been raised to double the minimum price, in consequence of railroad grants, they shall be computed to the States at the maximum price, and the number of acres proportionally diminished.

Sixth.   No State while in a condition of rebellion or insurrection against the government of the United States shall be entitled to the benefit of this act.

Seventh.   No State shall be entitled to the benefits of this act unless it shall express its acceptance thereof by its legislature within two years from the date of its approval by the President.

SEC. 6.   *And be it further enacted,* That land scrip issued under the provisions of this act shall not be subject to location until after the first day of January, one thousand eight hundred and sixty-three.

SEC. 7.   *And be it further enacted,* That the land officers shall receive the same fees for locating land scrip issued under the provisions of this act as is now allowed for the location of military bounty land warrants under existing laws: *Provided,* their maximum compensation shall not be thereby increased.

SEC. 8.   *And be it further enacted,* That the Governors of the several States to which scrip shall be issued under this act shall be required to report annually to Congress all sales made of such scrip until the whole shall be disposed of, the amount received for the same, and what appropriation has been made of the proceeds. Approved, July 2, 1862.

THEODORE RAWSON CRANE, Assistant Professor of History at the University of Denver, was born in Providence, Rhode Island, in 1929. He received his B.A. from Brown University, and his M.A. and Ph.D. from Harvard University. Before joining the faculty of the University of Denver, Professor Crane taught history at Dartmouth College and Duke University. He is completing a study of the life and thought of Francis Wayland and has begun the research for a history of Brown University since 1889.

Date Due